Key Stage 3
Age 13-14

CW00446740

Official
National Test Papers

English
Tests

London: The Stationery Office

Test material text © Qualifications and Curriculum Authority 1998

Introductory text © The Stationery Office 1999

Text p. vii – vii © The Times 1999

All rights reserved.
Applications for reproduction should be made in the first instance to The Stationery Office.

First published 1998
Second impression 1999

ISBN 0 11 370063 6

The Stationery Office is grateful for permission to use copyright material from the following:

Extracts from *Operation Wolf* reproduced with the permission of the Born Free Foundation. Text and illustration (cubs and single wolf) taken from BFF Literature 1993.

'Family Portrait' illustration reproduced with the permission of Jeff and Sue Turner/BBC Natural History Unit

Published by The Stationery Office and available from:

The Publications Centre
(mail, telephone and fax orders only)
PO Box 276, London SW8 5DT
General enquiries 0171 873 0011
Telephone orders 0171 873 9090
Fax orders 0171 873 8200

The Stationery Office Bookshops
123 Kingsway, London WC2B 6PQ
0171 242 6393 Fax 0171 242 6394
68-69 Bull Street, Birmingham B4 6AD
0121 236 9696 Fax 0121 236 9699
33 Wine Street, Bristol BS1 2BQ
0117 926 4306 Fax 0117 929 4515
9-21 Princess Street, Manchester M60 8AS
0161 834 7201 Fax 0161 833 0634
16 Arthur Street, Belfast BT1 4GD
01232 238451 Fax 01232 235401
The Stationery Office Oriel Bookshop
The Friary, Cardiff CF1 4AA
01222 395548 Fax 01222 384347
71 Lothian Road, Edinburgh EH3 9AZ
0131 228 4181 Fax 0131 622 7017

The Stationery Office's Accredited Agents
(see Yellow Pages)

and through good booksellers

Key Stage Tests

English, Key Stage 3, Age 13–14

Contents

Introduction v

The tests and how they help your child vi

Preparing for the tests vii

How to use this book ix

Guidance on administering the tests xi

Paper 1, 1998 Levels 4–7

    Question Paper (7 pages)

    Answer Booklet (8 pages)

Paper 2, 1998 Levels 4–7. Shakespeare Play

    Question Paper (7 pages)

    Scenes from the Plays (44 pages)

    Answer Booklet (8 pages)

Mark Scheme for Papers 1 and 2, 1998 Levels 4–7 (191 pages)

Introduction

This is one of three books which will help you work with your child to prepare for the tests almost all children take in Year 9 at the end of Key Stage 3 at about age 14. Using them will also give you some information about what your child knows in English, mathematics and science – known as the core subjects of the National Curriculum.

This book helps you and your child practise the English tests. The other two books help practise the mathematics and the science tests.

There are a number of books in the shops which set out to do this. Why are these books the best?

■ First, these are the only ones to contain last year's actual tests. When you and your child work through each book, you will be using the actual tests which children took last year. In 1999 the test questions will be different but the general appearance of the tests will be much the same.

■ Second, you can be sure that the help and advice which surrounds the tests is as useful as possible. It has been written in liaison with the Qualifications and Curriculum Authority, the official body which produces the tests and advises the Government on the National Curriculum.

The three books contain last year's tests which were taken by 14-year-olds. Using them gives your child a chance to get used to the tests and how to take them. They will also tell you more about how your child is doing in three key subjects, So they are one of the best ways you can help your child make progress.

The tests and how they help your child

Finding out what children know and can do is an important part of their education. It:

- helps teachers produce better plans and better classroom teaching;
- helps children think about their own learning;
- gives you information about your child;
- helps you help your child at home;
- builds up a picture of how well schools are doing.

This information is gained in three main ways.

1   Day by day, month by month, term by term, your child's teachers build up a picture of your child through the work they mark and through watching your child at work in the classroom.

    When you get your child's report each year and see your child's teacher in school at an open evening, you will receive a summary of this information.

2   At the ages of 7, 11 and 14 your child's work is assessed more formally. Your child's teachers will use the records they have made and make judgements about how your child is doing against the National Curriculum; this is called Teacher Assessment.

3   At the same time your child will also take the national tests in English, mathematics and science – except for the 7-year-olds, who do not have a science test. Almost every child in the country in those age groups take the same tests. Although they do not test everything, they cover some of the most important work your child has done in school in each of the three subjects.

    When the tests have been marked, your child will be awarded a 'level ' in each subject, based on how they performed in the tests. Both the Teacher Assessment levels and the test levels have to be given to you as part of the school's report.

Preparing for the tests

by John O'Leary, Education Editor of *The Times*.

Tests at the end of Key Stage 3 give parents and pupils their last chance to gauge progress before the onset of GCSE. They can be an invaluable guide to areas of strength and weakness, as well as providing an opportunity to polish up that all-important exam technique.

Although the results will not be used for league tables, they do give parents a check on a school's standards at a stage of education which inspectors have often found weak. Schools are obliged not only to publish national curriculum test results, but to set them in a national context.

As the last national tests before GCSE, the Key Stage 3 tests give 14-year-olds the chance to try out their revision skills in an arena which will not affect their long-term prospects. This book allows them to focus their work on the right areas and to plan for the type of questions they will face in the spring.

Assessment now takes place in all national curriculum subjects, but formal tests are limited to the core subjects of English, maths and science. The sample questions in this book are all taken from last year's tests, which will be similar this time.

Schools will run their own revision classes, but a little extra familiarisation, using the test examples, will aid this process. It will also show parents, for whom the tests will be unchartered territory, some of the concepts their children should have mastered by the age of 14.

There is no right or wrong way to prepare for these or any other tests. What suits one child may be quite wrong for another. But there are some basic points that hold good for most examinees, whatever the subject.

Thinking ahead

Perhaps the most important rule, whatever the subject, is not to leave revision to the last moment. Decide what you need to go over several weeks before the test, discuss it with your teacher and set aside some time. Find out what the school's revision plans are, and make sure that your's do not clash.

Do not revise in front of the television. A short period of concentrated work is worth hours shared with *Neighbours* or *Top of the Pops*. Find somewhere quiet, if possible, and do not allow yourself to be distracted.

Use the test examples to get an idea of what will be required in the test, but do not assume that your questions will be in the same areas. Make sure you are confident about all the main topics that you have covered.

In the week of the test

Divide your time between the different subjects, concentrating on weaknesses.
Use the practice questions in this book, but do not overdo last-minute revision:
you want to be alert for the test itself.

On the day

Make sure you have any materials needed for the test and that you are on time.
Then try to relax. In the end, the tests are just another step on the way to GCSE.

How to use this book

What is being tested?

This book contains last year's tests in English for 14-year-olds. There are two papers.

The National Curriculum for English is divided into three sections (or Attainment Targets):

1   **Speaking and Listening;**

2   **Reading;**

3   **Writing.**

The tests for 14-year-olds cover sections 2 and 3 at Levels 4–7.

How you can help your child prepare for the English test

■   Be encouraging and supportive, so that your child is confident about the tests.

■   Use this book to give confidence about what to expect in terms of format.

■   Talk with your child's teacher about how you can help your child improve, so that you can support and build on the work done in class.

■   Be interested in your child's work – in reading and writing. Try not to nag or be critical.

■   Talk with your child about classwork, stories, newspaper articles, television and radio programmes, current events.

Above all, encourage your child to read, and to read widely, non-fiction as well as stories, and lots of different authors. Share the reading with your child. Talk about stories: what happens and why, what the characters do, what they are like, is it a good story – would you recommend it to others? Remember though, there may be little point in encouraging your child to read if they never see you reading.

What to do next

Ask the teacher how you can best help your child. Be open and honest with the teachers and, if you have concerns, share them. They know your child well and are used to answering questions from parents. But don't leave it till the last minute.

Remember to encourage the use of dictionaries and encyclopaedias, as well as other information books, newspapers and word games. Encourage your child to write, not just stories but other things like letters, poems and plays, and to think about writing for different people and purposes.

Don't let your own worries about tests – if you have them – pass on to your child.

Hints for your child on taking the test

1   Listen carefully to the teacher's instructions and follow them exactly.

2   Read the questions carefully.

3   If you are not sure, ask for help. Your teacher can't tell you the answers, but will be able to help you understand what it is you have to do.

4   Don't try to write out the test in full, but plan in outline for the major points. Remember, the end is just as important as the beginning and the middle.

5   Use the reading time for the test fully. Read carefully and thoroughly, but don't spend too long on any words that might be unfamiliar. Carry on reading, and sometimes the meaning of the word will become clear, even if you don't know it to begin with.

Guidance on administering the tests

■ You should try to maintain appropriate test conditions by ensuring that your child is able to work undisturbed.

■ Have ruled A4 paper available if your child completes an answer booklet and asks for extra paper.

■ Make sure your child sees the 'Remember' section on the front cover of the test paper.

■ Give appropriate time reminders, for example, half way through the test and again 10 minutes before the end. Further guidance for each paper is given below.

■ Dictionaries or word lists (either monolingual or bilingual) are **not allowed** in the English tests.

Before the tests begin you should go through the instructions on the front of the question paper and advise your child on how to use his or her time.

Paper 1

■ Paper 1 lasts 1 hour 30 minutes and you should allow your child a further 15 minutes reading time at the beginning of the test to read and annotate the question paper, although they should not start to write in their answer booklets.

■ Advise your child to spend about 50 minutes on Sections A and B, and about 40 minutes on Section C.

■ Your child should answer **all** questions in Sections A and B, but only **one** question in Section C.

You may explain, where relevant, that a question refers to particular lines in a passage and that the sentence in bold print is the question. The prompts will help your child to understand what to do and which areas to cover in the answer. If your child asks how much to write, you should refer to the number of marks allocated to the question and the areas indicated by the prompts and make it clear, where appropriate, that quite a detailed answer is required. Attention may be drawn to instructions such as 'support your ideas with words and phrases from the passage'. This could be explained as picking out words from the passage, putting them in quotation marks, and explaining how they support the answer.

Paper 2: Shakespeare Play

- Paper 2 lasts 1 hour 15 minutes

- Remind your child to answer one task only on one scene from the play he or she has studied. You may explain the structure of the task: the first sentence sets the scene, the task itself is in bold print, and the prompts will help your child to think about the areas that need to be covered and how to structure the answer.

- Draw your child's attention to the fact that the shaded flashes on the page edges in the booklet of Shakespeare scenes correspond to those in the paper, in order to help in finding the correct scene.

- Advise your child to spend the first 10-15 minutes of the test reading the chosen scene, making notes on the task, and planning the answer.

Paper 1, 1998
Levels 4–7

Write your name and school on the front cover of your answer booklet.

Remember

- At the beginning of this test, you have 15 minutes to read the paper and make notes, but you must not start to write your answers until you are told to do so.

- Then you have 1 hour 30 minutes to write your answers.

- You should answer **all** of the questions in Sections A and B. Then choose **one** question only from Section C.

- You should spend **about 10 minutes on question 1**
  20 minutes on question 2
  20 minutes on question 3
  40 minutes on question 4.

- Check your work carefully.

  Ask if you are not sure what to do.

Read the following story.

Then answer question 1 and question 2.

This story is set in New Zealand. It is about a school trip to a science museum. At the museum the attendant puts a live snake around the neck of the teacher, Miss Aitcheson.

The story is told by a woman who happens to be visiting the museum at the same time.

I made my way to the main hall. Children, sitting in rows on canvas chairs. A class from a city school, under the control of an elderly teacher. A museum attendant holding a basket, and all eyes gazing at the basket.

'Oh,' I said. 'Is this a private lesson? Is it all right for me to be here?'   5

The attendant was brisk. 'Surely. We're having a lesson in snake-handling,' he said. 'It's something new. Get the children young and teach them that every snake they meet is not to be killed. People seem to think that every snake has to be knocked on the head. So we're getting them young and teaching them.'   10

'May I watch?' I said.

'Surely. This is a common grass snake. No harm, no harm at all. Teach the children to learn the feel of them, to lose their fear.'

He turned to the teacher. 'Now, Miss - Mrs -' he said.

'Miss Aitcheson.'   15

He lowered his voice. 'The best way to get through to the children is to start with teacher,' he said to Miss Aitcheson. 'If they see you're not afraid, then they won't be.'

She must be near retiring age, I thought. A city woman. Never handled a snake in her life. Her face was pale. She just managed to drag the   20
fear from her eyes to some place in their depths, where it lurked like a dark stain. Surely the attendant and the children noticed?

'It's harmless,' the attendant said. He'd been working with snakes for years.

Her eyes faced the lighted exit. I saw her fear. The exit light blinked, 25
hooded. The children, none of whom had ever touched a live snake,
were sitting hushed, waiting for the drama to begin; one or two looked
afraid as the attendant withdrew a green snake about three feet long
from the basket and with a swift movement, before the teacher could
protest, draped it around her neck and stepped back, admiring and 30
satisfied.

'There,' he said to the class. 'Your teacher has a snake around her
neck and she's not afraid.'

Miss Aitcheson stood rigid; she seemed to be holding her breath.

'Teacher's not afraid, are you?' the attendant persisted. He leaned 35
forward, pronouncing judgement on her, while she suddenly jerked
her head and lifted her hands in panic to get rid of the snake. Then,
seeing the children watching her, she whispered, 'No, I'm not afraid.
Of course not.' She looked around her.

'Of course not,' she repeated sharply. 40

I could see her defeat and helplessness. The attendant seemed
unaware, as if his perception had grown a reptilian covering.

'See, Miss Aitcheson's touching the snake. She's not afraid of it at all.'

As everyone watched, she touched the snake. Her fingers recoiled.
She touched it again. 45

'See, she's not afraid. Miss Aitcheson can stand there with a beautiful
snake around her neck and touch it and stroke it and not be afraid.'

The faces of the children were full of admiration for the teacher's bravery,
and yet there was a cruelly persistent tension; they were waiting,
waiting. 50

'We have to learn to love snakes,' the attendant said. 'Would someone
like to come out and stroke teacher's snake?'

Silence.

One shamefaced boy came forward. He stood petrified in front of the
teacher. 55

Turn over

3

'Touch it,' the attendant urged. 'It's a friendly snake. Teacher's wearing it around her neck and she's not afraid.'

The boy darted his hand forward, rested it lightly on the snake, and immediately withdrew his hand. Then he ran back to his seat. The children shrieked with glee. 60

'He's afraid,' someone said. 'He's afraid of the snake.'

The attendant soothed. 'We have to get used to them, you know. Grown-ups are not afraid of them, but we can understand that when you're small you might be afraid, and that's why we want you to learn to love them. Isn't that right, Miss Aitcheson? Isn't that right? Now who 65 else is going to be brave enough to touch teacher's snake?'

Two girls came out. They stood hand in hand, side by side and stared at the snake and then at Miss Aitcheson.

I wondered when the torture would end. The two little girls did not touch the snake, but they smiled at it and spoke to it and Miss Aitcheson smiled 70 at them and whispered how brave they were.

'Just a minute,' the attendant said. 'There's really no need to be brave. It's not a question of bravery. The snake is *harmless*, absolutely *harmless*. Where's the bravery when the snake is harmless?'

Suddenly the snake moved around to face Miss Aitcheson and thrust its 75 flat head toward her cheek. She gave a scream, flung up her hands, and tore the snake from her throat and threw it on the floor, and, rushing across the room, she collapsed into a small canvas chair and started to cry.

I didn't feel I should watch any longer. Some of the children began to 80 laugh, some to cry. The attendant picked up the snake and nursed it. Miss Aitcheson, recovering, sat helplessly exposed by the small piece of useless torture. It was not her fault she was city-bred, her eyes tried to tell us. She looked at the children, trying in some way to force their admiration and respect; they were shut against her. 85

You Are Now Entering the Human Heart by Janet Frame.

Answer question 1 and question 2. **Remember** *to spend less time on question 1 than the other questions.*

Refer to words and phrases in the passage to support your ideas.

1. **What impression do you get of the museum attendant's attitude towards snakes?**

    In your answer you should comment on:

    • the way the museum attendant talks about and handles the snake;

    • the way he sees his job.

    6 marks

2. **How does the writer make you feel increasingly sorry for Miss Aitcheson?**

    In your answer you should comment on:

    • the way Miss Aitcheson is described;

    • the way she reacts to having the snake around her neck;

    • the way the museum attendant and the children treat Miss Aitcheson;

    • the way the story ends and the writer's reaction to what happens.

    11 marks

Turn over

Section B

Read the information on page 8.

It is from a leaflet trying to persuade people to change their opinions about wolves.

Now answer question 3.

Refer to words and phrases from the leaflet to support your ideas.

3. **How does the leaflet try to change people's opinions about wolves?**

   In your answer you should comment on:

   - how the leaflet describes many people's feelings about wolves;

   - how the writer has selected information about wolves to persuade the reader;

   - the way words and layout are used to try to create a positive image of wolves;

   - whether you think the leaflet will succeed in changing people's opinions about wolves.

   11 marks

Section C

This section of the paper is a test of writing. You will be assessed on:

- *your ideas and the way you organise and express them;*
- *your ability to write clearly, using paragraphs and accurate grammar, spelling and punctuation.*

*Choose **ONE** of the following:*

4.   EITHER

     a)   Imagine you are a director of a new museum. (You can decide what is in the museum.)

               Write a letter to headteachers of schools in the area encouraging them to bring groups of pupils to visit the museum.

               Write an address for the museum at the top. Begin your letter *Dear Headteacher* and end it with *Yours faithfully* and your signature.

               In your letter you could write about:

- what the museum has to offer;
- why it is of educational value;
- why young people will enjoy a visit and learn from it;
- how to organise a trip there.

     OR

     b)   **Write about a frightening encounter with an animal.**

               You could:

- write about a real or imaginary event;
- try to build up a feeling of tension or suspense.

     OR

     c)   The leaflet you have read tries to change people's opinions about wolves.

               Imagine you have been given a chance to talk in a year assembly. Choose an issue you feel strongly about. (It does not need to be about animals.)

               Write your speech trying to persuade other people to support your views.

33 marks

THE WOLF

Once the most widespread mammal in the Northern Hemisphere, the wolf now stands on the brink of extinction in many countries. In others it has gone – possibly forever.

THREATS TO SURVIVAL

- Persecution by people
- Habitat destruction
- Competition with people for larger prey
- Hybridisation (cross-breeding between wolves and wild dogs)

In Britain it is over 250 years since the forests provided the last refuge for wolves trying to escape the all-out war that was waged against them.

What is it about this animal that, in some people, arouses such intense feelings of fear and hate? Yet those people who have studied this species hold wolves in deep respect, admiring their intelligence, devotion to family and skilled hunting abilities.

Buried deep in many people's subconscious is the 'fictional' wolf – the villain of myth and fairy tale. Add to this the competition between humans and wolves for food and land, and the result has been a long-running, one-sided battle which has sadly made the wolf one of nature's most misunderstood and persecuted animals.

How you can help

You can join Operation Wolf by becoming an adoptive wolf parent. To get your Adoption Pack, telephone xxxxx xxxxxx. (*Number supplied in original leaflet.*)

Family life

Wolves live in a tightly-knit group called a 'pack', bound by friendship, loyalty and need. They enjoy playing together and the security the pack offers. Pups are the focal point for the whole family with uncles and aunts all helping to provide food and care. Intelligent and friendly, the wolf is one of nature's most socially developed animals.

The key to the wolf's survival is harmony, which is made possible thanks to their elaborate ability to communicate. Techniques include scent-marking, a wide variety of facial expressions and body postures, not forgetting the wolf's trade mark – the beautiful eerie howl. This, however, is more than just a means of communication. Wolves often howl simply for the sheer joy of it.

Family portrait

WOLF FACTS

- The wolf is the largest of the *canidae* (dog) family
- All domestic dogs are descended from wolves
- Wolves prey on deer, wild boar, small rodents and berries!
- Fur is thick and a mixture of colours – grey, red, brown, black and white

Is it too late to save the wolf?

Over the last few decades the wolf has been the subject of many in-depth studies, all of which have uncovered evidence to help shatter the cruel illusion created by legend.

Slowly but surely the wolf's affectionate and loyal nature is being recognised. Their desperate attempts to survive in the remote areas to which they have been driven have led to a conservation challenge that aims to give the wolf the survival chance it deserves.

Paper 1, Levels 4–7 Answer Booklet

First Name _____

Last Name _____

School _____

Write your answers in this booklet.

You may ask for more paper if you need it.

Do not write in margin

Do not
write in
margin

You may use this page to plan your answer.

Paper 2, 1998
Levels 4–7
Shakespeare Play

Write your name and school on the front cover of your answer booklet.

Remember

- The test is 1 hour 15 minutes long.

- You should do **one** task on **one** of the following plays:

  Julius Caesar – do the task on page 2 **or** the task on page 3;
  A Midsummer Night's Dream – do the task on page 4 **or** the task on page 5;
  Romeo and Juliet – do the task on page 6 **or** the task on page 7

- Your work will be assessed for your knowledge and understanding of the play and the way you express your ideas.

- Check your work carefully.

- Ask if you are not sure what to do.

Choose *one* task.

If you have studied 'Julius Caesar' do either Task 1 or Task 2.

EITHER

Julius Caesar

Act 1 Scene 2, lines 1 - 214

TASK 1

In this scene Cassius seizes the opportunity to talk to Brutus about Caesar.

Comment in detail on the different ways Cassius tries to persuade Brutus to think the same way as he does.

Before you begin to write you should think about:

- why Cassius chooses this moment to speak to Brutus;

- the way Cassius uses his understanding of Brutus's character;

- the impression of Caesar that Cassius tries to give to Brutus;

- the different ways Cassius uses language to persuade Brutus.

Read the task again before you begin to write your answer.

OR

Julius Caesar

Act 4 Scene 3, lines 124 - 308

TASK 2

This scene takes place before the battle of Philippi and after the quarrel with Cassius.

Imagine you are Brutus. Write down and explain your thoughts and feelings at this tense and difficult time.

You could begin: *I know this is a turning point, for Rome and*
                                          for me ...

Before you begin to write you should decide what Brutus thought and felt about:

- the death of his wife, Portia;

- his conversations with Cassius;

- why the ghost appeared;

- the battle of Philippi that was soon going to take place.

Remember to write as if you are Brutus.

Read the task again before you begin to write your answer.

---

*Choose **one** task.*

If you have studied 'A Midsummer Night's Dream' do either Task 3 or Task 4.

EITHER

A Midsummer Night's Dream

Act 2 Scene 1, lines 1 - 185

TASK 3

Imagine you are going to direct this scene for your year group.

Explain how you want the fairies to play their parts and what you want to suggest to the audience about the fairy world.

Before you begin to write you should think about:

- what you would tell the pupils playing Oberon and Titania about how to play their parts;

- what you would say to the pupil playing Puck about his role;

- the atmosphere you want to create and how you would do this;

- the effects you would use to create the fairy world.

Read the task again before you begin to write your answer.

A Midsummer Night's Dream

Act 3 Scene 2, lines 122 - 344

TASK 4

In this scene Helena's world is turned upside-down.

Imagine you are Helena. Write down your thoughts and the confusion you feel as you run away.

You could begin: *I am totally confused! I can trust no one ...*

Before you begin to write you should think about Helena's views on:

- the strange way Lysander and Demetrius have been behaving;

- Hermia's unexpected behaviour and the terrible names Hermia has called her;

- the reasons the characters have been speaking and behaving in this way;

- how her friendship with Hermia has changed.

Remember to write as if you are Helena.

Read the task again before you begin to write your answer.

*Choose **one** task.*

If you have studied 'Romeo and Juliet' do either Task 5 or Task 6.

EITHER

Romeo and Juliet

Act 2 Scene 4, line 82 to end of Scene 5

TASK 5

In these scenes the Nurse is the messenger between Romeo and Juliet.

What do you learn about the Nurse and how does her character add to the humour in these scenes?

Before you begin to write you should think about:

- the Nurse's feelings about her involvement in the secret arrangements;

- how the differences in the way the Nurse speaks to Romeo and Mercutio are amusing;

- the humour in the different ways Mercutio, Romeo and Juliet treat the Nurse;

- how the Nurse's behaviour towards Juliet adds humour.

Read the task again before you begin to write your answer.

OR

Romeo and Juliet

Act 3 Scene 1

TASK 6

From the beginning of this scene the audience realises that the feud between the families will lead to tragedy.

Explain in detail how you think Shakespeare builds up tension and excitement in this scene.

Before you begin to write you should think about:

- how tension is created in the opening of the scene (lines 1 - 48);

- how Mercutio's and Tybalt's words and actions build up tension and excitement;

- how Romeo's words and behaviour add to the tension;

- how the arrival of the Prince adds to the tension at the end of the scene.

Read the task again before you begin to write your answer.

Romeo and Juliet

END OF TEST

Scenes from Shakespeare Plays

for use with

Paper 2, 1998 Levels 4–7

Look at the question paper and choose which task to do.

The scene for each task is printed in this booklet.

Look below to find the page where the scene begins.

Julius Caesar

Act 1 Scene 2	page 4
Act 4 Scene 3	page 10

A Midsummer Night's Dream

Act 2 Scene 1	page 19
Act 3 Scene 2	page 24

Romeo and Juliet

Act 2 Scenes 4-5	page 32
Act 3 Scene 1	page 39

Julius Caesar

Act 1 Scene 2

**You will find the task for this scene
on page 2 of your question paper.**

and

Act 4 Scene 3

**You will find the task for this scene
on page 3 of your question paper.**

JULIUS CAESAR

Act 1 Scene 2, lines 1 - 214

Enter CAESAR, ANTONY *for the course,* CALPURNIA, *Portia, Decius, Cicero,* BRUTUS, CASSIUS, CASCA, *a* SOOTHSAYER, [*a great crowd following*]; *after them Murellus and Flavius*

CAESAR	Calpurnia.
CASCA	Peace ho, Caesar speaks.
CAESAR	Calpurnia.
CALPURNIA	Here, my lord.
CAESAR	Stand you directly in Antonio's way When he doth run his course. Antonio.
ANTONY	Caesar, my lord.

5

CAESAR	Forget not in your speed, Antonio, To touch Calpurnia, for our elders say The barren, touchèd in this holy chase, Shake off their sterile curse.
ANTONY	I shall remember: When Caesar says, 'Do this', it is performed.

10

CAESAR	Set on, and leave no ceremony out.
SOOTHSAYER	Caesar!
CAESAR	Ha? Who calls?
CASCA	Bid every noise be still – peace yet again!
CAESAR	Who is it in the press that calls on me? I hear a tongue shriller than all the music Cry 'Caesar!' Speak, Caesar is turned to hear.

15

SOOTHSAYER	Beware the Ides of March.
CAESAR	What man is that?
BRUTUS	A soothsayer bids you beware the Ides of March.
CAESAR	Set him before me, let me see his face.

20

4

CASSIUS	Fellow, come from the throng, look upon Caesar.
CAESAR	What say'st thou to me now? Speak once again.
SOOTHSAYER	Beware the Ides of March.
CAESAR	He is a dreamer, let us leave him. Pass.

Sennet. Exeunt [all but] Brutus and Cassius

CASSIUS	Will you go see the order of the course?	25
BRUTUS	Not I.	
CASSIUS	I pray you, do.	
BRUTUS	I am not gamesome: I do lack some part	
	Of that quick spirit that is in Antony.	
	Let me not hinder, Cassius, your desires;	30
	I'll leave you.	
CASSIUS	Brutus, I do observe you now of late:	
	I have not from your eyes that gentleness	
	And show of love as I was wont to have.	
	You bear too stubborn and too strange a hand	35
	Over your friend that loves you.	
BRUTUS	Cassius,	
	Be not deceived. If I have veiled my look	
	I turn the trouble of my countenance	
	Merely upon myself. Vexèd I am	
	Of late with passions of some difference,	40
	Conceptions only proper to myself,	
	Which give some soil, perhaps, to my behaviours.	
	But let not therefore my good friends be grieved	
	(Among which number, Cassius, be you one)	
	Nor construe any further my neglect	45
	Than that poor Brutus, with himself at war,	
	Forgets the shows of love to other men.	
CASSIUS	Then, Brutus, I have much mistook your passion,	
	By means whereof this breast of mine hath buried	
	Thoughts of great value, worthy cogitations.	50
	Tell me, good Brutus, can you see your face?	
BRUTUS	No, Cassius, for the eye sees not itself	
	But by reflection, by some other things.	

CASSIUS 'Tis just,
And it is very much lamented, Brutus, 55
That you have no such mirrors as will turn
Your hidden worthiness into your eye
That you might see your shadow. I have heard
Where many of the best respect in Rome
(Except immortal Caesar), speaking of Brutus 60
And groaning underneath this age's yoke,
Have wished that noble Brutus had his eyes.

BRUTUS Into what dangers would you lead me, Cassius,
That you would have me seek into myself
For that which is not in me? 65

CASSIUS Therefore, good Brutus, be prepared to hear.
And since you know you cannot see yourself
So well as by reflection, I, your glass,
Will modestly discover to yourself
That of yourself which you yet know not of. 70
And be not jealous on me, gentle Brutus,
Were I a common laughter, or did use
To stale with ordinary oaths my love
To every new protester. If you know
That I do fawn on men and hug them hard 75
And after scandal them, or if you know
That I profess myself in banqueting
To all the rout, then hold me dangerous.

Flourish and shout

BRUTUS What means this shouting? I do fear the people
Choose Caesar for their king.

CASSIUS   Ay, do you fear it? 80
Then must I think you would not have it so.

BRUTUS I would not, Cassius, yet I love him well.
But wherefore do you hold me here so long?
What is it that you would impart to me?
If it be aught toward the general good, 85
Set honour in one eye and death i'th'other
And I will look on both indifferently.
For let the gods so speed me as I love
The name of honour more than I fear death.

CASSIUS I know that virtue to be in you, Brutus, 90
As well as I do know your outward favour.
Well, honour is the subject of my story:
I cannot tell what you and other men

Think of this life, but for my single self
I had as lief not be as live to be   95
In awe of such a thing as I myself.
I was born free as Caesar, so were you;
We both have fed as well, and we can both
Endure the winter's cold as well as he.
For once, upon a raw and gusty day,   100
The troubled Tiber chafing with her shores,
Caesar said to me, 'Dar'st thou, Cassius, now
Leap in with me into this angry flood
And swim to yonder point?' Upon the word,
Accoutred as I was, I plungèd in   105
And bade him follow; so indeed he did.
The torrent roared, and we did buffet it
With lusty sinews, throwing it aside
And stemming it with hearts of controversy.
But ere we could arrive the point proposed,   110
Caesar cried, 'Help me, Cassius, or I sink!'
Ay, as Aeneas, our great ancestor,
Did from the flames of Troy upon his shoulder
The old Anchises bear, so from the waves of Tiber
Did I the tired Caesar. And this man   115
Is now become a god, and Cassius is
A wretched creature and must bend his body
If Caesar carelessly but nod on him.
He had a fever when he was in Spain,
And when the fit was on him I did mark   120
How he did shake. 'Tis true, this god did shake,
His coward lips did from their colour fly,
And that same eye whose bend doth awe the world
Did lose his lustre. I did hear him groan,
Ay, and that tongue of his that bade the Romans   125
Mark him and write his speeches in their books,
'Alas', it cried, 'give me some drink, Titinius',
As a sick girl. Ye gods, it doth amaze me
A man of such a feeble temper should
So get the start of the majestic world   130
And bear the palm alone.

Shout. Flourish

BRUTUS   Another general shout!
                I do believe that these applauses are
                For some new honours that are heaped on Caesar.

CASSIUS   Why, man, he doth bestride the narrow world   135
                Like a Colossus, and we petty men
                Walk under his huge legs and peep about
                To find ourselves dishonourable graves.
                Men at some time are masters of their fates:

The fault, dear Brutus, is not in our stars   *140*
But in ourselves, that we are underlings.
Brutus and Caesar: what should be in that 'Caesar'?
Why should that name be sounded more than yours?
Write them together, yours is as fair a name;
Sound them, it doth become the mouth as well;   *145*
Weigh them, it is as heavy; conjure with 'em,
'Brutus' will start a spirit as soon as 'Caesar'.
Now in the names of all the gods at once,
Upon what meat doth this our Caesar feed
That he is grown so great? Age, thou art shamed!   *150*
Rome, thou hast lost the breed of noble bloods!
When went there by an age since the great flood
But it was famed with more than with one man?
When could they say, till now, that talked of Rome,
That her wide walks encompassed but one man?   *155*
Now is it Rome indeed and room enough
When there is in it but one only man.
O, you and I have heard our fathers say
There was a Brutus once that would have brooked
Th'eternal devil to keep his state in Rome   *160*
As easily as a king.

BRUTUS   That you do love me, I am nothing jealous;
                What you would work me to, I have some aim.
                How I have thought of this, and of these times,
                I shall recount hereafter. For this present,   *165*
                I would not (so with love I might entreat you)
                Be any further moved. What you have said
                I will consider; what you have to say
                I will with patience hear and find a time
                Both meet to hear and answer such high things. *170*
                Till then, my noble friend, chew upon this:
                Brutus had rather be a villager
                Than to repute himself a son of Rome
                Under these hard conditions as this time
                Is like to lay upon us.   *175*

CASSIUS   I am glad that my weak words
                Have struck but thus much show of fire from Brutus.

                Enter CAESAR *and his* TRAIN

BRUTUS   The games are done and Caesar is returning.

CASSIUS   As they pass by, pluck Casca by the sleeve
                And he will (after his sour fashion) tell you   *180*
                What hath proceeded worthy note today.

8

BRUTUS	I will do so. But look you, Cassius,	
	The angry spot doth glow on Caesar's brow	
	And all the rest look like a chidden train:	
	Calpurnia's cheek is pale, and Cicero	*185*
	Looks with such ferret and such fiery eyes	
	As we have seen him in the Capitol,	
	Being crossed in conference by some senators.	

CASSIUS	Casca will tell us what the matter is.	

CAESAR	Antonio.	*190*

ANTONY	Caesar.	

CAESAR	Let me have men about me that are fat,	
	Sleek-headed men and such as sleep a-nights.	
	Yond Cassius has a lean and hungry look,	
	He thinks too much: such men are dangerous.	*195*

ANTONY	Fear him not, Caesar, he's not dangerous,	
	He is a noble Roman and well given.	

CAESAR	Would he were fatter! But I fear him not.	
	Yet if my name were liable to fear	
	I do not know the man I should avoid	*200*
	So soon as that spare Cassius. He reads much,	
	He is a great observer, and he looks	
	Quite through the deeds of men. He loves no plays,	
	As thou dost, Antony, he hears no music;	
	Seldom he smiles, and smiles in such a sort	*205*
	As if he mocked himself and scorned his spirit	
	That could be moved to smile at any thing.	
	Such men as he be never at heart's ease	
	Whiles they behold a greater than themselves,	
	And therefore are they very dangerous.	*210*
	I rather tell thee what is to be feared	
	Than what I fear: for always I am Caesar.	
	Come on my right hand, for this ear is deaf,	
	And tell me truly what thou think'st of him.	

Sennet. Exeunt Caesar and his train

JULIUS CAESAR

Act 4 Scene 3, lines 124 - 308

Enter a POET, [LUCILIUS and Titinius]

POET	Let me go in to see the generals.	
	There is some grudge between 'em, 'tis not meet	125
	They be alone.	
LUCILIUS	You shall not come to them.	
POET	Nothing but death shall stay me.	
CASSIUS	How now, what's the matter?	
POET	For shame, you generals, what do you mean?	130
	Love and be friends, as two such men should be,	
	For I have seen more years, I'm sure, than ye.	
CASSIUS	Ha, ha, how vildly doth this cynic rhyme!	
BRUTUS	Get you hence, sirrah; saucy fellow, hence!	
CASSIUS	Bear with him, Brutus, 'tis his fashion.	135
BRUTUS	I'll know his humour when he knows his time.	
	What should the wars do with these jigging fools?	
	Companion, hence!	
CASSIUS	Away, away, be gone!	

Exit Poet

BRUTUS	Lucilius and Titinius, bid the commanders	
	Prepare to lodge their companies tonight.	140
CASSIUS	And come yourselves, and bring Messala with you	
	Immediately to us.	

[Exeunt Lucilius and Titinius]

BRUTUS	[*To Lucius within*] Lucius, a bowl of wine!
CASSIUS	I did not think you could have been so angry.
BRUTUS	O Cassius, I am sick of many griefs.

CASSIUS	Of your philosophy you make no use If you give place to accidental evils.	*145*
BRUTUS	No man bears sorrow better. Portia is dead.	
CASSIUS	Ha? Portia?	
BRUTUS	She is dead.	
CASSIUS	How scaped I killing when I crossed you so? O insupportable and touching loss! Upon what sickness?	*150*
BRUTUS	Impatient of my absence, And grief that young Octavius with Mark Antony Have made themselves so strong – for with her death That tidings came. With this she fell distract And, her attendants absent, swallowed fire.	*155*
CASSIUS	And died so?	
BRUTUS	Even so.	
CASSIUS	O ye immortal gods!	

Enter BOY [LUCIUS] *with wine and tapers*

| BRUTUS | Speak no more of her. Give me a bowl of wine.
In this I bury all unkindness, Cassius.   *Drinks* | |
| CASSIUS | My heart is thirsty for that noble pledge.
Fill, Lucius, till the wine o'erswell the cup,
I cannot drink too much of Brutus' love.   *[Drinks]* | *160* |

                                                       [Exit Lucius]

Enter TITINIUS *and* MESSALA

BRUTUS	Come in, Titinius; welcome, good Messala. Now sit we close about this taper here And call in question our necessities.	*165*
CASSIUS	Portia, art thou gone?	
BRUTUS	No more, I pray you. Messala, I have here receivèd letters That young Octavius and Mark Antony Come down upon us with a mighty power, Bending their expedition toward Philippi.	*170*

MESSALA	Myself have letters of the selfsame tenor.
BRUTUS	With what addition?
MESSALA	That by proscription and bills of outlawry Octavius, Antony, and Lepidus Have put to death an hundred senators.

175

BRUTUS	Therein our letters do not well agree: Mine speak of seventy senators that died By their proscriptions, Cicero being one.
CASSIUS	Cicero one?
MESSALA	Cicero is dead, And by that order of proscription. Had you your letters from your wife, my lord?

180

BRUTUS	No, Messala.
MESSALA	Nor nothing in your letters writ of her?
BRUTUS	Nothing, Messala.
MESSALA	That, methinks, is strange.
BRUTUS	Why ask you? Hear you aught of her in yours?

185

MESSALA	No, my lord.
BRUTUS	Now as you are a Roman tell me true.
MESSALA	Then like a Roman bear the truth I tell, For certain she is dead, and by strange manner.
BRUTUS	Why, farewell, Portia. We must die, Messala. With meditating that she must die once, I have the patience to endure it now.

190

MESSALA	Even so, great men great losses should endure.
CASSIUS	I have as much of this in art as you, But yet my nature could not bear it so.

195

BRUTUS	Well, to our work alive. What do you think Of marching to Philippi presently?
CASSIUS	I do not think it good.
BRUTUS	Your reason?

CASSIUS   This it is:
　　　　　　　　'Tis better that the enemy seek us,
　　　　　　　　So shall he waste his means, weary his soldiers,   *200*
　　　　　　　　Doing himself offence, whilst we, lying still,
　　　　　　　　Are full of rest, defence, and nimbleness.

BRUTUS   Good reasons must of force give place to better:
　　　　　　　　The people 'twixt Philippi and this ground
　　　　　　　　Do stand but in a forced affection,   *205*
　　　　　　　　For they have grudged us contribution.
　　　　　　　　The enemy, marching along by them,
　　　　　　　　By them shall make a fuller number up,
　　　　　　　　Come on refreshed, new added, and encouraged,
　　　　　　　　From which advantage shall we cut him off   *210*
　　　　　　　　If at Philippi we do face him there,
　　　　　　　　These people at our back.

CASSIUS   Hear me, good brother.

BRUTUS   Under your pardon. You must note beside
　　　　　　　　That we have tried the utmost of our friends,
　　　　　　　　Our legions are brimful, our cause is ripe;   *215*
　　　　　　　　The enemy increaseth every day,
　　　　　　　　We, at the height, are ready to decline.
　　　　　　　　There is a tide in the affairs of men
　　　　　　　　Which, taken at the flood, leads on to fortune;
　　　　　　　　Omitted, all the voyage of their life   *220*
　　　　　　　　Is bound in shallows and in miseries.
　　　　　　　　On such a full sea are we now afloat,
　　　　　　　　And we must take the current when it serves
　　　　　　　　Or lose our ventures.

CASSIUS   Then with your will go on,
　　　　　　　　We'll along ourselves and meet them at Philippi.   *225*

BRUTUS   The deep of night is crept upon our talk,
　　　　　　　　And nature must obey necessity,
　　　　　　　　Which we will niggard with a little rest.
　　　　　　　　There is no more to say?

CASSIUS   No more. Good night.
　　　　　　　　Early tomorrow will we rise and hence.   *230*

BRUTUS	Lucius!

Enter LUCIUS

My gown.

[*Exit Lucius*]

Farewell, good Messala.
Good night, Titinius. Noble, noble Cassius,
Good night and good repose.

CASSIUS   O my dear brother!
This was an ill beginning of the night.
Never come such division 'tween our souls!   235
Let it not, Brutus.

Enter LUCIUS *with the gown*

BRUTUS   Everything is well.

CASSIUS   Good night, my lord.

BRUTUS   Good night, good brother.

TITINIUS AND   Good night, Lord Brutus.
MESSALA

BRUTUS   Farewell every one.

Exeunt [*Cassius, Titinius, Messala*]

Give me the gown. Where is thy instrument?

LUCIUS   Here in the tent.

BRUTUS   What, thou speak'st drowsily.   240
Poor knave, I blame thee not, thou art o'erwatched.
Call Claudio and some other of my men,
I'll have them sleep on cushions in my tent.

LUCIUS   Varrus and Claudio!

Enter VARRUS *and* CLAUDIO

VARRUS   Calls my lord?   245

BRUTUS	I pray you, sirs, lie in my tent and sleep, It may be I shall raise you by and by On business to my brother Cassius.	
VARRUS	So please you, we will stand and watch your pleasure.	
BRUTUS	I will not have it so. Lie down, good sirs, It may be I shall otherwise bethink me.	250

[Varrus and Claudio lie down]

	Look, Lucius, here's the book I sought for so, I put it in the pocket of my gown.	
LUCIUS	I was sure your lordship did not give it me.	
BRUTUS	Bear with me, good boy, I am much forgetful. Canst thou hold up thy heavy eyes awhile And touch thy instrument a strain or two?	255
LUCIUS	Ay, my lord, an't please you.	
BRUTUS	It does, my boy. I trouble thee too much, but thou art willing.	
LUCIUS	It is my duty, sir.	260
BRUTUS	I should not urge thy duty past thy might, I know young bloods look for a time of rest.	
LUCIUS	I have slept, my lord, already.	
BRUTUS	It was well done and thou shalt sleep again, I will not hold thee long. If I do live I will be good to thee.	265

Music, and a song

	This is a sleepy tune. O murd'rous slumber, Layest thou thy leaden mace upon my boy, That plays thee music? Gentle knave, good night, I will not do thee so much wrong to wake thee. If thou dost nod thou break'st thy instrument. I'll take it from thee and, good boy, good night. Let me see, let me see, is not the leaf turned down Where I left reading? Here it is, I think.	270

15

Enter the GHOST OF CAESAR

How ill this taper burns! Ha, who comes here?   275
I think it is the weakness of mine eyes
That shapes this monstrous apparition.
It comes upon me. Art thou any thing?
Art thou some god, some angel, or some devil,
That mak'st my blood cold and my hair to stare?   280
Speak to me what thou art.

GHOST   Thy evil spirit, Brutus.

BRUTUS   Why com'st thou?

GHOST   To tell thee thou shalt see me at Philippi.

BRUTUS   Well, then I shall see thee again?

GHOST   Ay, at Philippi.   285

BRUTUS   Why, I will see thee at Philippi then.

                                             [*Exit Ghost*]

Now I have taken heart thou vanishest.
Ill spirit, I would hold more talk with thee.
Boy, Lucius! Varrus! Claudio! Sirs, awake!
Claudio!   290

LUCIUS   The strings, my lord, are false.

BRUTUS   He thinks he still is at his instrument.
Lucius, awake!

LUCIUS   My lord?

BRUTUS   Didst thou dream, Lucius, that thou so cried'st out?   295

LUCIUS   My lord, I do not know that I did cry.

BRUTUS   Yes, that thou didst. Didst thou see anything?

LUCIUS   Nothing, my lord.

BRUTUS   Sleep again, Lucius. Sirrah Claudio!
[*To Varrus*] Fellow, thou, awake!   300

VARRUS   My lord?

CLAUDIO   My lord?

BRUTUS   Why did you so cry out, sirs, in your sleep?

BOTH   Did we, my lord?

BRUTUS   Ay. Saw you anything?

VARRUS   No, my lord, I saw nothing.

CLAUDIO   Nor I, my lord.   305

BRUTUS   Go and commend me to my brother Cassius.
Bid him set on his powers betimes before,
And we will follow.

BOTH   It shall be done, my lord.

Exeunt

A Midsummer Night's Dream

Act 2 Scene 1

**You will find the task for this scene
on page 4 of your question paper.**

and

Act 3 Scene 2

**You will find the task for this scene
on page 5 of your question paper.**

A MIDSUMMER NIGHT'S DREAM

Act 2 Scene 1, lines 1 - 185

The wood

Enter a FAIRY *at one door, and* [PUCK, *or*] ROBIN GOODFELLOW
at another.

PUCK

How now, spirit; whither wander you?

FAIRY

    Over hill, over dale,
        Thorough bush, thorough briar,
    Over park, over pale,
        Thorough flood, thorough fire;   *5*
    I do wander everywhere
    Swifter than the moon's sphere;
    And I serve the Fairy Queen,
    To dew her orbs upon the green.
    The cowslips tall her pensioners be;   *10*
    In their gold coats spots you see –
    Those be rubies, fairy favours,
    In those freckles live their savours.
        I must go seek some dewdrops here,
        And hang a pearl in every cowslip's ear.   *15*
Farewell, thou lob of spirits; I'll be gone.
Our Queen and all her elves come here anon.

PUCK

The King doth keep his revels here tonight.
Take heed the Queen come not within his sight,
For Oberon is passing fell and wrath,   *20*
Because that she as her attendant hath
A lovely boy stol'n from an Indian king;
She never had so sweet a changeling,
And jealous Oberon would have the child
Knight of his train, to trace the forests wild.   *25*
But she perforce withholds the lovèd boy,
Crowns him with flowers, and makes him all her joy.
And now they never meet in grove or green,
By fountain clear or spangled starlight sheen,
But they do square, that all their elves for fear   *30*
Creep into acorn cups and hide them there.

FAIRY	Either I mistake your shape and making quite,	
	Or else you are that shrewd and knavish sprite	
	Called Robin Goodfellow. Are not you he	
	That frights the maidens of the villagery,	35
	Skim milk, and sometimes labour in the quern,	
	And bootless make the breathless housewife churn,	
	And sometime make the drink to bear no barm,	
	Mislead night-wanderers, laughing at their harm?	
	Those that 'Hobgoblin' call you, and 'Sweet Puck',	40
	You do their work, and they shall have good luck.	
	Are not you he?	

PUCK	Thou speakest aright;	
	I am that merry wanderer of the night.	
	I jest to Oberon, and make him smile	
	When I a fat and bean-fed horse beguile,	45
	Neighing in likeness of a filly foal;	
	And sometime lurk I in a gossip's bowl	
	In very likeness of a roasted crab,	
	And when she drinks, against her lips I bob,	
	And on her withered dewlap pour the ale.	50
	The wisest aunt, telling the saddest tale,	
	Sometime for threefoot stool mistaketh me;	
	Then slip I from her bum, down topples she,	
	And 'Tailor' cries, and falls into a cough;	
	And then the whole choir hold their hips and loffe,	55
	And waxen in their mirth, and neeze, and swear	
	A merrier hour was never wasted there.	
	But room, Fairy: here comes Oberon.	

FAIRY	And here my mistress. Would that he were gone!	

Enter [OBERON,] *the King of Fairies, at one door, with his train;*
and [TITANIA,] *the Queen, at another with hers.*

OBERON	Ill met by moonlight, proud Titania!	60

TITANIA	What, jealous Oberon? Fairies, skip hence.	
	I have forsworn his bed and company.	

OBERON	Tarry, rash wanton! Am not I thy lord?	

TITANIA	Then I must be thy lady. But I know	
	When thou hast stol'n away from Fairyland,	65
	And in the shape of Corin sat all day	
	Playing on pipes of corn, and versing love	
	To amorous Phillida. Why art thou here	
	Come from the farthest step of India? –	
	But that, forsooth, the bouncing Amazon,	70
	Your buskined mistress and your warrior love,	
	To Theseus must be wedded; and you come	
	To give their bed joy and prosperity.	

OBERON How canst thou thus, for shame, Titania,
Glance at my credit with Hippolyta, 75
Knowing I know thy love to Theseus?
Didst not thou lead him through the glimmering night
From Perigenia, whom he ravishèd,
And make him with fair Aegles break his faith,
With Ariadne, and Antiopa? 80

TITANIA These are the forgeries of jealousy:
And never since the middle summer's spring
Met we on hill, in dale, forest, or mead,
By pavèd fountain or by rushy brook,
Or in the beachèd margent of the sea 85
To dance our ringlets to the whistling wind,
But with thy brawls thou hast disturbed our sport.
Therefore the winds, piping to us in vain,
As in revenge have sucked up from the sea
Contagious fogs; which, falling in the land, 90
Hath every pelting river made so proud
That they have overborne their continents.
The ox hath therefore stretched his yoke in vain,
The ploughman lost his sweat, and the green corn
Hath rotted ere his youth attained a beard. 95
The fold stands empty in the drownèd field,
And crows are fatted with the murrion flock;
The nine-men's-morris is filled up with mud,
And the quaint mazes in the wanton green
For lack of tread are undistinguishable. 100
The human mortals want their winter cheer;
No night is now with hymn or carol blessed.
Therefore the moon, the governess of floods,
Pale in her anger, washes all the air,
That rheumatic diseases do abound; 105
And thorough this distemperature we see

The seasons alter; hoary-headed frosts
Fall in the fresh lap of the crimson rose,
And on old Hiems' thin and icy crown
An odorous chaplet of sweet summer buds   *110*
Is, as in mockery, set. The spring, the summer,
The childing autumn, angry winter change
Their wonted liveries, and the mazèd world
By their increase now knows not which is which.
And this same progeny of evils comes   *115*
From our debate, from our dissension.
We are their parents and original.

OBERON   Do you amend it, then: it lies in you.
                Why should Titania cross her Oberon?
                I do but beg a little changeling boy   *120*
                To be my henchman.

TITANIA   Set your heart at rest.
                The fairy land buys not the child of me.
                His mother was a votress of my order,
                And in the spicèd Indian air by night
                Full often hath she gossiped by my side,   *125*
                And sat with me on Neptune's yellow sands
                Marking th'embarkèd traders on the flood,
                When we have laughed to see the sails conceive
                And grow big-bellied with the wanton wind;
                Which she, with pretty and with swimming gait *130*
                Following (her womb then rich with my young squire),
                Would imitate, and sail upon the land
                To fetch me trifles, and return again
                As from a voyage, rich with merchandise.
                But she, being mortal, of that boy did die, *135*
                And for her sake do I rear up her boy;
                And for her sake I will not part with him.

OBERON   How long within this wood intend you stay?

TITANIA   Perchance till after Theseus' wedding day.
                If you will patiently dance in our round,   *140*
                And see our moonlight revels, go with us:
                If not, shun me, and I will spare your haunts.

OBERON   Give me that boy, and I will go with thee.

TITANIA   Not for thy fairy kingdom! Fairies, away.
                We shall chide downright if I longer stay.   *145*

                                Exeunt [*Titania and her train*]

22

OBERON   Well, go thy way. Thou shalt not from this grove
            Till I torment thee for this injury.
            My gentle Puck, come hither. Thou rememberest
            Since once I sat upon a promontory,
            And heard a mermaid on a dolphin's back   *150*
            Uttering such dulcet and harmonious breath
            That the rude sea grew civil at her song,
            And certain stars shot madly from their spheres
            To hear the sea-maid's music?

PUCK   I remember.

OBERON   That very time I saw (but thou couldst not)   *155*
            Flying between the cold moon and the earth
            Cupid all armed: a certain aim he took
            At a fair vestal thronèd by the west,
            And loosed his loveshaft smartly from his bow
            As it should pierce a hundred thousand hearts;   *160*
            But I might see young Cupid's fiery shaft
            Quenched in the chaste beams of the watery moon;
            And the imperial votress passèd on
            In maiden meditation, fancy-free.
            Yet marked I where the bolt of Cupid fell: *165*
            It fell upon a little western flower,
            Before, milk-white; now purple with love's wound:
            And maidens call it 'love-in-idleness'.
            Fetch me that flower, the herb I showed thee once;
            The juice of it on sleeping eyelids laid   *170*
            Will make or man or woman madly dote
            Upon the next live creature that it sees.
            Fetch me this herb, and be thou here again
            Ere the leviathan can swim a league.

PUCK   I'll put a girdle round about the earth   *175*
            In forty minutes!

                                                              [*Exit*]

OBERON   Having once this juice
            I'll watch Titania when she is asleep,
            And drop the liquor of it in her eyes:
            The next thing then she, waking, looks upon –
            Be it on lion, bear, or wolf, or bull,   *180*
            On meddling monkey, or on busy ape –
            She shall pursue it with the soul of love.
            And ere I take this charm from off her sight
            (As I can take it with another herb)
            I'll make her render up her page to me.   *185*

23

A MIDSUMMER NIGHT'S DREAM

Act 3 Scene 2, lines 122 - 344

Enter LYSANDER *and* HELENA.

LYSANDER	Why should you think that I should woo in scorn?	
	Scorn and derision never come in tears.	
	Look when I vow, I weep; and vows so born,	
	In their nativity all truth appears.	*125*
	How can these things in me seem scorn to you,	
	Bearing the badge of faith to prove them true?	
HELENA	You do advance your cunning more and more.	
	When truth kills truth, O devilish-holy fray!	
	These vows are Hermia's. Will you give her o'er?	*130*
	Weigh oath with oath, and you will nothing weigh;	
	Your vows to her and me, put in two scales,	
	Will even weigh, and both as light as tales.	
LYSANDER	I had no judgement when to her I swore.	
HELENA	Nor none, in my mind, now you give her o'er.	*135*
LYSANDER	Demetrius loves her, and he loves not you.	
DEMETRIUS	(*Waking.*)	
	O Helen, goddess, nymph, perfect, divine!	
	To what, my love, shall I compare thine eyne?	
	Crystal is muddy! O, how ripe in show	
	Thy lips, those kissing cherries, tempting grow!	*140*
	That pure congealèd white, high Taurus' snow,	
	Fanned with the eastern wind, turns to a crow	
	When thou hold'st up thy hand. O, let me kiss	
	This princess of pure white, this seal of bliss!	
HELENA	O spite! O Hell! I see you all are bent	*145*
	To set against me for your merriment.	
	If you were civil, and knew courtesy,	
	You would not do me thus much injury.	
	Can you not hate me, as I know you do,	
	But you must join in souls to mock me too?	*150*
	If you were men, as men you are in show,	
	You would not use a gentle lady so,	
	To vow, and swear, and superpraise my parts,	
	When I am sure you hate me with your hearts.	
	You both are rivals, and love Hermia;	*155*

24

And now both rivals to mock Helena.
A trim exploit, a manly enterprise,
To conjure tears up in a poor maid's eyes
With your derision! None of noble sort
Would so offend a virgin, and extort   160
A poor soul's patience, all to make you sport.

LYSANDER   You are unkind, Demetrius: be not so,
For you love Hermia — this you know I know —
And here with all good will, with all my heart,
In Hermia's love I yield you up my part;   165
And yours of Helena to me bequeath,
Whom I do love, and will do till my death.

HELENA   Never did mockers waste more idle breath.

DEMETRIUS   Lysander, keep thy Hermia; I will none.
If e'er I loved her, all that love is gone.   170
My heart to her but as guest-wise sojourned,
And now to Helen is it home returned,
There to remain.

LYSANDER   Helen, it is not so.

DEMETRIUS   Disparage not the faith thou dost not know,
Lest to thy peril thou aby it dear.   175
Look where thy love comes: yonder is thy dear.

Enter Hermia.

HERMIA   Dark night, that from the eye his function takes,
The ear more quick of apprehension makes;
Wherein it doth impair the seeing sense
It pays the hearing double recompense.   180
Thou art not by mine eye, Lysander, found;
Mine ear, I thank it, brought me to thy sound.
But why unkindly didst thou leave me so?

LYSANDER   Why should he stay whom love doth press to go?

HERMIA   What love could press Lysander from my side?   185

LYSANDER   Lysander's love, that would not let him bide,
Fair Helena — who more engilds the night
Than all yon fiery oes and eyes of light.
[*To Hermia*] Why seek'st thou me? Could not this make
        thee know
The hate I bare thee made me leave thee so?   190

HERMIA   You speak not as you think; it cannot be.

25

HELENA	Lo, she is one of this confederacy!	
	Now I perceive they have conjoined all three	
	To fashion this false sport in spite of me.	
	Injurious Hermia, most ungrateful maid,	*195*
	Have you conspired, have you with these contrived	
	To bait me with this foul derision?	
	Is all the counsel that we two have shared,	
	The sisters' vows, the hours that we have spent	
	When we have chid the hasty-footed time	*200*
	For parting us — O, is all forgot?	
	All schooldays' friendship, childhood innocence?	
	We, Hermia, like two artificial gods	
	Have with our needles created both one flower,	
	Both on one sampler, sitting on one cushion,	*205*
	Both warbling of one song, both in one key,	
	As if our hands, our sides, voices, and minds	
	Had been incorporate. So we grew together	
	Like to a double cherry, seeming parted,	
	But yet an union in partition,	*210*
	Two lovely berries moulded on one stem;	
	So with two seeming bodies but one heart,	
	Two of the first, like coats in heraldry,	
	Due but to one, and crownèd with one crest.	
	And will you rent our ancient love asunder,	*215*
	To join with men in scorning your poor friend?	
	It is not friendly, 'tis not maidenly.	
	Our sex, as well as I, may chide you for it,	
	Though I alone do feel the injury.	

| HERMIA | I am amazèd at your passionate words. | *220* |
| | I scorn you not; it seems that you scorn me. | |

HELENA	Have you not set Lysander, as in scorn,	
	To follow me, and praise my eyes and face?	
	And made your other love, Demetrius,	
	Who even but now did spurn me with his foot,	*225*
	To call me goddess, nymph, divine and rare,	
	Precious, celestial? Wherefore speaks he this	
	To her he hates? And wherefore doth Lysander	
	Deny your love, so rich within his soul,	
	And tender me, forsooth, affection,	*230*
	But by your setting on, by your consent?	
	What though I be not so in grace as you,	
	So hung upon with love, so fortunate,	
	But miserable most, to love unloved:	
	This you should pity rather than despise.	*235*

| HERMIA | I understand not what you mean by this. | |

HELENA	Ay, do! Persever, counterfeit sad looks,
	Make mouths upon me when I turn my back,
	Wink each at other, hold the sweet jest up.
	This sport, well carried, shall be chronicled. *240*
	If you have any pity, grace, or manners,
	You would not make me such an argument.
	But fare ye well. 'Tis partly my own fault,
	Which death or absence soon shall remedy.
LYSANDER	Stay, gentle Helena: hear my excuse, *245*
	My love, my life, my soul, fair Helena!
HELENA	O, excellent!
HERMIA	[*To Lysander*] Sweet, do not scorn her so.
DEMETRIUS	If she cannot entreat, I can compel.
LYSANDER	Thou canst compel no more than she entreat;
	Thy threats have no more strength than her weak prayers. *250*
	Helen, I love thee, by my life, I do:
	I swear by that which I will lose for thee
	To prove him false that says I love thee not.
DEMETRIUS	I say I love thee more than he can do.
LYSANDER	If thou say so, withdraw, and prove it too. *255*
DEMETRIUS	Quick, come.
HERMIA	Lysander, whereto tends all this?
LYSANDER	Away, you Ethiop!
DEMETRIUS	No, no, sir,
	Seem to break loose, take on as you would follow,
	But yet come not. You are a tame man, go.
LYSANDER	Hang off, thou cat, thou burr! Vile thing, let loose, *260*
	Or I will shake thee from me like a serpent.
HERMIA	Why are you grown so rude? What change is this,
	Sweet love?
LYSANDER	Thy love? — out, tawny Tartar, out;
	Out, loathed medicine! O hated potion, hence!
HERMIA	Do you not jest?
HELENA	Yes, sooth, and so do you. *265*

LYSANDER   Demetrius, I will keep my word with thee.

DEMETRIUS   I would I had your bond, for I perceive
            A weak bond holds you. I'll not trust your word.

LYSANDER   What? Should I hurt her, strike her, kill her dead?
            Although I hate her, I'll not harm her so.   270

HERMIA   What? Can you do me greater harm than hate?
            Hate me? Wherefore? O me, what news, my love?
            Am not I Hermia? Are not you Lysander?
            I am as fair now as I was erewhile.
            Since night you loved me; yet since night you left me.   275
            Why then, you left me — O, the gods forbid! —
            In earnest, shall I say?

LYSANDER   Ay, by my life;
            And never did desire to see thee more.
            Therefore be out of hope, of question, of doubt;
            Be certain, nothing truer — 'tis no jest   280
            That I do hate thee and love Helena.

HERMIA   [To Helena]
            O me, you juggler, you canker-blossom,
            You thief of love! What, have you come by night
            And stol'n my love's heart from him?

HELENA   Fine, i'faith!
            Have you no modesty, no maiden shame,   285
            No touch of bashfulness? What, will you tear
            Impatient answers from my gentle tongue?
            Fie, fie, you counterfeit, you puppet, you!

HERMIA   'Puppet'? Why so? — Ay, that way goes the game.
            Now I perceive that she hath made compare   290
            Between our statures; she hath urged her height,
            And with her personage, her tall personage,
            Her height, forsooth, she hath prevailed with him.
            And are you grown so high in his esteem
            Because I am so dwarfish and so low?   295
            How low am I, thou painted maypole? Speak!
            How low am I? I am not yet so low
            But that my nails can reach unto thine eyes.

HELENA   I pray you, though you mock me, gentlemen,
            Let her not hurt me. I was never curst;   300
            I have no gift at all in shrewishness.
            I am a right maid for my cowardice;

Let her not strike me. You perhaps may think
Because she is something lower than myself
That I can match her.

HERMIA   Lower? Hark, again!   *305*

HELENA   Good Hermia, do not be so bitter with me.
              I evermore did love you, Hermia,
              Did ever keep your counsels, never wronged you,
              Save that in love unto Demetrius
              I told him of your stealth unto this wood.   *310*
              He followed you; for love I followed him,
              But he hath chid me hence, and threatened me
              To strike me, spurn me, nay, to kill me too.
              And now, so you will let me quiet go,
              To Athens will I bear my folly back,   *315*
              And follow you no further. Let me go;
              You see how simple and how fond I am.

HERMIA   Why, get you gone! Who is't that hinders you?

HELENA   A foolish heart that I leave here behind.

HERMIA   What, with Lysander?

HELENA   With Demetrius.   *320*

LYSANDER   Be not afraid; she shall not harm thee, Helena.

DEMETRIUS   No, sir. She shall not, though you take her part.

HELENA   O, when she is angry she is keen and shrewd;
              She was a vixen when she went to school,
              And though she be but little, she is fierce.   *325*

HERMIA   Little again? Nothing but low and little?
              Why will you suffer her to flout me thus?
              Let me come to her.

LYSANDER   Get you gone, you dwarf,
              You minimus of hindering knot-grass made,
              You bead, you acorn.

DEMETRIUS   You are too officious   *330*
              In her behalf that scorns your services.
              Let her alone: speak not of Helena,
              Take not her part; for if thou dost intend
              Never so little show of love to her,
              Thou shalt aby it.

LYSANDER   Now she holds me not —   *335*
                    Now follow, if thou dur'st, to try whose right,
                    Of thine or mine, is most in Helena.

DEMETRIUS   Follow? Nay, I'll go with thee, cheek by jowl.

                                        Exeunt Lysander and Demetrius

HERMIA   You, mistress, all this coil is 'long of you.
                    Nay, go not back.

HELENA   I will not trust you, I,   *340*
                    Nor longer stay in your curst company.
                    Your hands than mine are quicker for a fray;
                    My legs are longer, though, to run away!   [*Exit*]

HERMIA   I am amazed, and know not what to say.   *Exit*

Romeo and Juliet

Act 2 Scenes 4 - 5

**You will find the task for these scenes
on page 6 of your question paper.**

and

Act 3 Scene 1

**You will find the task for this scene
on page 7 of your question paper.**

ROMEO AND JULIET

Act 2 Scene 4, line 82 to the end of Scene 5

ROMEO   Here's goodly gear!

        Enter NURSE *and her man* [PETER].

        A sail, a sail!

MERCUTIO   Two, two: a shirt and a smock.

NURSE   Peter!   *85*

PETER   Anon.

NURSE   My fan, Peter.

MERCUTIO   Good Peter, to hide her face, for her fan's the fairer face.

NURSE   God ye good morrow, gentlemen.

MERCUTIO   God ye good den, fair gentlewoman.   *90*

NURSE   Is it good den?

MERCUTIO   'Tis no less, I tell ye, for the bawdy hand of the dial is now upon the prick of noon.

NURSE   Out upon you, what a man are you?

ROMEO   One, gentlewoman, that God hath made, himself to mar. *95*

NURSE   By my troth, it is well said: 'for himself to mar', quoth'a? Gentlemen, can any of you tell me where I may find the young Romeo?

ROMEO   I can tell you, but young Romeo will be older when you have found him than he was when you sought him: I am the youngest *100* of that name, for fault of a worse.

NURSE   You say well.

MERCUTIO   Yea, is the worst well? Very well took, i'faith, wisely, wisely.

| NURSE | If you be he, sir, I desire some confidence with you. | 105 |

| BENVOLIO | She will indite him to some supper. | |

| MERCUTIO | A bawd, a bawd, a bawd! So ho! | |

| ROMEO | What hast thou found? | |

| MERCUTIO | No hare, sir, unless a hare, sir, in a lenten pie, that is something stale and hoar ere it be spent. | 110 |

[*He walks by them and sings.*]

An old hare hoar,
And an old hare hoar,
Is very good meat in Lent;
But a hare that is hoar
Is too much for a score,   115
When it hoars ere it be spent.
Romeo, will you come to your father's? We'll to dinner thither.

| ROMEO | I will follow you. | |

| MERCUTIO | Farewell, ancient lady, farewell, lady, [*Singing.*] 'lady, lady'. | 120 |

Exeunt [*Mercutio and Benvolio*]

| NURSE | I pray you, sir, what saucy merchant was this that was so full of his ropery? | |

| ROMEO | A gentleman, Nurse, that loves to hear himself talk, and will speak more in a minute than he will stand to in a month. | |

| NURSE | And 'a speak any thing against me, I'll take him down, and 'a were lustier than he is, and twenty such Jacks; and if I cannot, I'll find those that shall. Scurvy knave, I am none of his flirt-gills, I am none of his skains-mates. [*She turns to Peter, her man.*] And thou must stand by too and suffer every knave to use me at his pleasure! | 125 |

| PETER | I saw no man use you at his pleasure; if I had, my weapon should quickly have been out. I warrant you, I dare draw as soon as another man, if I see occasion in a good quarrel, and the law on my side. | 130 |

NURSE	Now afore God, I am so vexed that every part about me quivers. Scurvy knave! Pray you, sir, a word: and as I told you, my young lady bid me enquire you out; what she bid me say, I will keep to myself. But first let me tell ye, if ye should lead her in a fool's paradise, as they say, it were a very gross kind of behaviour, as they say; for the gentlewoman is young; and therefore, if you should deal double with her, truly it were an ill thing to be offered to any gentlewoman, and very weak dealing.	135
		140
ROMEO	Nurse, commend me to thy lady and mistress. I protest unto thee –	
NURSE	Good heart, and i'faith I will tell her as much. Lord, Lord, she will be a joyful woman.	
ROMEO	What wilt thou tell her, Nurse? thou dost not mark me.	145
NURSE	I will tell her, sir, that you do protest, which, as I take it, is a gentleman-like offer.	
ROMEO	Bid her devise Some means to come to shrift this afternoon, And there she shall at Friar Lawrence' cell Be shrived and married. Here is for thy pains.	150
NURSE	No truly, sir, not a penny.	
ROMEO	Go to, I say you shall.	
NURSE	This afternoon, sir? Well, she shall be there.	
ROMEO	And stay, good Nurse, behind the abbey wall: Within this hour my man shall be with thee, And bring thee cords made like a tackled stair, Which to the high top-gallant of my joy Must be my convoy in the secret night. Farewell, be trusty, and I'll quit thy pains. Farewell, commend me to thy mistress.	155
		160
NURSE	Now God in heaven bless thee! Hark you, sir.	
ROMEO	What say'st thou, my dear Nurse?	
NURSE	Is your man secret? Did you ne'er hear say, 'Two may keep counsel, putting one away'?	165
ROMEO	'Warrant thee, my man's as true as steel.	

NURSE	Well, sir, my mistress is the sweetest lady – Lord, Lord! when 'twas a little prating thing – O, there is a nobleman in town, one Paris, that would fain lay knife aboard; but she, good soul, had as lieve see a toad, a very toad, as see him. I anger her sometimes, *170* and tell her that Paris is the properer man, but I'll warrant you, when I say so, she looks as pale as any clout in the versal world. Doth not rosemary and Romeo begin both with a letter?
ROMEO	Ay, Nurse, what of that? Both with an R.
NURSE	Ah, mocker, that's the dog-name. R is for the – no, I know it *175* begins with some other letter – and she hath the prettiest sententious of it, of you and rosemary, that it would do you good to hear it.
ROMEO	Commend me to thy lady.
NURSE	Ay, a thousand times.

[Exit Romeo]

Peter!

PETER	Anon.	*180*

NURSE	[*Handing him her fan.*] Before and apace.

Exit [after Peter]

Act 2 Scene 5

Capulet's mansion

Enter JULIET.

JULIET   The clock struck nine when I did send the Nurse;
           In half an hour she promised to return.
           Perchance she cannot meet him: that's not so.
           O, she is lame! Love's heralds should be thoughts,
           Which ten times faster glides than the sun's beams,   *5*
           Driving back shadows over low'ring hills;
           Therefore do nimble-pinioned doves draw Love,
           And therefore hath the wind-swift Cupid wings.
           Now is the sun upon the highmost hill
           Of this day's journey, and from nine till twelve   *10*
           Is three long hours, yet she is not come.
           Had she affections and warm youthful blood,
           She would be as swift in motion as a ball;
           My words would bandy her to my sweet love,
           And his to me.   *15*
           But old folks, many feign as they were dead,
           Unwieldy, slow, heavy, and pale as lead.

Enter NURSE [with PETER].

           O God, she comes! O honey Nurse, what news?
           Hast thou met with him? Send thy man away.

NURSE   Peter, stay at the gate.   *20*

                                                        [*Exit Peter*]

JULIET   Now, good sweet Nurse – O Lord, why look'st thou sad?
           Though news be sad, yet tell them merrily;
           If good, thou shamest the music of sweet news
           By playing it to me with so sour a face.

NURSE   I am a-weary, give me leave a while.   *25*
           Fie, how my bones ache! What a jaunce have I!

JULIET   I would thou hadst my bones, and I thy news.
           Nay, come, I pray thee speak, good, good Nurse, speak.

NURSE   Jesu, what haste! can you not stay a while?
           Do you not see that I am out of breath?   *30*

JULIET	How art thou out of breath, when thou hast breath
	To say to me that thou art out of breath?
	The excuse that thou dost make in this delay
	Is longer than the tale thou dost excuse.
	Is thy news good or bad? Answer to that. 35
	Say either, and I'll stay the circumstance:
	Let me be satisfied, is't good or bad?
NURSE	Well, you have made a simple choice, you know not how to
	choose a man: Romeo? no, not he; though his face be better than
	any man's, yet his leg excels all men's, and for a hand and a foot 40
	and a body, though they be not to be talked on, yet they are past
	compare. He is not the flower of courtesy, but I'll warrant him, as
	gentle as a lamb. Go thy ways, wench, serve God. What, have you
	dined at home?
JULIET	No, no! But all this did I know before. 45
	What says he of our marriage, what of that?
NURSE	Lord, how my head aches! what a head have I!
	It beats as it would fall in twenty pieces.
	My back a't'other side – ah, my back, my back!
	Beshrew your heart for sending me about 50
	To catch my death with jauncing up and down!
JULIET	I'faith, I am sorry that thou art not well.
	Sweet, sweet, sweet Nurse, tell me, what says my love?
NURSE	Your love says, like an honest gentleman,
	And a courteous, and a kind, and a handsome, 55
	And I warrant a virtuous – Where is your mother?
JULIET	Where is my mother? why, she is within,
	Where should she be? How oddly thou repliest:
	'Your love says, like an honest gentleman,
	"Where is your mother?" '
NURSE	O God's lady dear, 60
	Are you so hot? Marry come up, I trow;
	Is this the poultice for my aching bones?
	Henceforward do your messages yourself.
JULIET	Here's such a coil! Come, what says Romeo?
NURSE	Have you got leave to go to shrift today? 65
JULIET	I have.

NURSE   Then hie you hence to Friar Lawrence' cell,
                         There stays a husband to make you a wife.
                         Now comes the wanton blood up in your cheeks,
                         They'll be in scarlet straight at any news.   *70*
                         Hie you to church, I must another way,
                         To fetch a ladder, by the which your love
                         Must climb a bird's nest soon when it is dark.
                         I am the drudge, and toil in your delight;
                         But you shall bear the burden soon at night.   *75*
                         Go, I'll to dinner, hie you to the cell.

JULIET   Hie to high fortune! Honest Nurse, farewell.

                                                    Exeunt

ROMEO AND JULIET

Act 3 Scene 1

Enter MERCUTIO [*and his* PAGE], BENVOLIO, *and* MEN.

BENVOLIO
I pray thee, good Mercutio, let's retire:
The day is hot, the Capels are abroad,
And if we meet we shall not scape a brawl,
For now, these hot days, is the mad blood stirring.

MERCUTIO
Thou art like one of these fellows that, when he enters the   5
confines of a tavern, claps me his sword upon the table, and says
'God send me no need of thee!'; and by the operation of the second
cup draws him on the drawer, when indeed there is no need.

BENVOLIO
Am I like such a fellow?

MERCUTIO
Come, come, thou art as hot a Jack in thy mood as any in   10
Italy, and as soon moved to be moody, and as soon moody to be
moved.

BENVOLIO
And what to?

MERCUTIO
Nay, and there were two such, we should have none shortly,
for one would kill the other. Thou? why, thou wilt quarrel with   15
a man that hath a hair more or a hair less in his beard than thou
hast; thou wilt quarrel with a man for cracking nuts, having no other
reason but because thou hast hazel eyes. What eye but such an eye
would spy out such a quarrel? Thy head is as full of quarrels as
an egg is full of meat, and yet thy head hath been beaten as addle   20
as an egg for quarrelling. Thou hast quarrelled with a man for
coughing in the street, because he hath wakened thy dog that hath
lain asleep in the sun. Didst thou not fall out with a tailor for
wearing his new doublet before Easter? with another for tying his
new shoes with old riband? and yet thou wilt tutor me from   25
quarrelling?

BENVOLIO
And I were so apt to quarrel as thou art, any man should
buy the fee-simple of my life for an hour and a quarter.

MERCUTIO
The fee-simple? O simple!

Enter TYBALT, PETRUCHIO, *and others.*

39

BENVOLIO	By my head, here comes the Capulets.	*30*
MERCUTIO	By my heel, I care not.	
TYBALT	Follow me close, for I will speak to them. Gentlemen, good den, a word with one of you.	
MERCUTIO	And but one word with one of us? couple it with something, make it a word and a blow.	*35*
TYBALT	You shall find me apt enough to that, sir, and you will give me occasion.	
MERCUTIO	Could you not take some occasion without giving?	
TYBALT	Mercutio, thou consortest with Romeo.	
MERCUTIO	Consort? what, dost thou make us minstrels? And thou make minstrels of us, look to hear nothing but discords. Here's my fiddlestick, here's that shall make you dance. 'Zounds, consort!	*40*
BENVOLIO	We talk here in the public haunt of men: Either withdraw unto some private place, Or reason coldly of your grievances, Or else depart; here all eyes gaze on us.	*45*
MERCUTIO	Men's eyes were made to look, and let them gaze; I will not budge for no man's pleasure, I.	

Enter ROMEO.

TYBALT	Well, peace be with you, sir, here comes my man.	
MERCUTIO	But I'll be hanged, sir, if he wear your livery. Marry, go before to field, he'll be your follower; Your worship in that sense may call him man.	*50*
TYBALT	Romeo, the love I bear thee can afford No better term than this: thou art a villain.	
ROMEO	Tybalt, the reason that I have to love thee Doth much excuse the appertaining rage To such a greeting. Villain am I none; Therefore farewell, I see thou knowest me not.	*55*
TYBALT	Boy, this shall not excuse the injuries That thou hast done me, therefore turn and draw.	*60*

Romeo and Juliet

ROMEO
I do protest I never injuried thee,
But love thee better than thou canst devise,
Till thou shalt know the reason of my love;
And so, good Capulet, which name I tender
As dearly as mine own, be satisfied.   65

MERCUTIO
O calm, dishonourable, vile submission!
'Alla stoccata' carries it away. [*Draws.*]
Tybalt, you rat-catcher, will you walk?

TYBALT
What wouldst thou have with me?

MERCUTIO
Good King of Cats, nothing but one of your nine lives that   70
I mean to make bold withal, and as you shall use me hereafter,
dry-beat the rest of the eight. Will you pluck your sword out of
his pilcher by the ears? Make haste, lest mine be about your ears
ere it be out.

TYBALT
I am for you. [*Drawing.*]   75

ROMEO
Gentle Mercutio, put thy rapier up.

MERCUTIO
Come, sir, your 'passado'.

[*They fight.*]

ROMEO
Draw, Benvolio, beat down their weapons.
Gentlemen, for shame forbear this outrage!
Tybalt, Mercutio, the Prince expressly hath   80
Forbid this bandying in Verona streets.
        [*Romeo steps between them.*]
Hold, Tybalt! Good Mercutio!
    [*Tybalt under Romeo's arm thrusts Mercutio in.*]
                    Away Tybalt [*with his followers*]

MERCUTIO
                                I am hurt.
A plague a'both houses! I am sped.
Is he gone and hath nothing?

BENVOLIO
                            What, art thou hurt?

MERCUTIO
Ay, ay, a scratch, a scratch, marry, 'tis enough.   85
Where is my page? Go, villain, fetch a surgeon.

[*Exit Page*]

ROMEO
Courage, man, the hurt cannot be much.

41

| MERCUTIO | No, 'tis not so deep as a well, nor so wide as a church-door, but 'tis enough, 'twill serve. Ask for me tomorrow, and you shall find me a grave man. I am peppered, I warrant, for this world. A plague a'both your houses! 'Zounds, a dog, a rat, a mouse, a cat, to scratch a man to death! a braggart, a rogue, a villain, that fights by the book of arithmetic. Why the dev'l came you between us? I was hurt under your arm. | 90 |

| ROMEO | I thought all for the best. | 95 |

| MERCUTIO | Help me into some house, Benvolio, Or I shall faint. A plague a'both your houses! They have made worms' meat of me. I have it, And soundly too. Your houses! |

Exit [with Benvolio]

| ROMEO | This gentleman, the Prince's near ally, My very friend, hath got this mortal hurt In my behalf; my reputation stained With Tybalt's slander – Tybalt, that an hour Hath been my cousin. O sweet Juliet, Thy beauty hath made me effeminate, And in my temper softened valour's steel! | 100

105 |

Enter Benvolio.

| BENVOLIO | O Romeo, Romeo, brave Mercutio is dead. That gallant spirit hath aspired the clouds, Which too untimely here did scorn the earth. |

| ROMEO | This day's black fate on moe days doth depend, This but begins the woe others must end. | 110 |

[Enter Tybalt.]

| BENVOLIO | Here comes the furious Tybalt back again. |

| ROMEO | Again, in triumph, and Mercutio slain? Away to heaven, respective lenity, And fire-eyed fury be my conduct now! Now, Tybalt, take the 'villain' back again That late thou gavest me, for Mercutio's soul Is but a little way above our heads, Staying for thine to keep him company: Either thou or I, or both, must go with him. | 115

120 |

| TYBALT | Thou wretched boy, that didst consort him here, Shalt with him hence. |

ROMEO   This shall determine that.

They fight; Tybalt falls.

BENVOLIO   Romeo, away, be gone!
                The citizens are up, and Tybalt slain.
                Stand not amazed, the Prince will doom thee death   125
                If thou art taken. Hence be gone, away!

ROMEO   O, I am fortune's fool.

BENVOLIO   Why dost thou stay?

                                                Exit Romeo

Enter Citizens [as OFFICERS of the Watch].

OFFICER   Which way ran he that killed Mercutio?
                Tybalt, that murderer, which way ran he?

BENVOLIO   There lies that Tybalt.

OFFICER   Up, sir, go with me;   130
                I charge thee in the Prince's name obey.

*Enter PRINCE, old MONTAGUE, CAPULET, their WIVES,
                and all.*

PRINCE   Where are the vile beginners of this fray?

BENVOLIO   O noble Prince, I can discover all
                The unlucky manage of this fatal brawl;
                There lies the man, slain by young Romeo,   135
                That slew thy kinsman, brave Mercutio.

LADY CAPULET   Tybalt, my cousin! O my brother's child!
                O Prince! O husband! O, the blood is spilled
                Of my dear kinsman. Prince, as thou art true,
                For blood of ours, shed blood of Montague.   140
                O cousin, cousin!

PRINCE   Benvolio, who began this bloody fray?

BENVOLIO   Tybalt, here slain, whom Romeo's hand did slay.
                Romeo, that spoke him fair, bid him bethink
                How nice the quarrel was, and urged withal   145
                Your high displeasure; all this, utterèd
                With gentle breath, calm look, knees humbly bowed,

43

Could not take truce with the unruly spleen
Of Tybalt deaf to peace, but that he tilts
With piercing steel at bold Mercutio's breast,   *150*
Who, all as hot, turns deadly point to point,
And with a martial scorn, with one hand beats
Cold death aside, and with the other sends
It back to Tybalt, whose dexterity
Retorts it. Romeo he cries aloud,   *155*
'Hold, friends! friends, part!' and swifter than his tongue,
His agile arm beats down their fatal points,
And 'twixt them rushes; underneath whose arm
An envious thrust from Tybalt hit the life
Of stout Mercutio, and then Tybalt fled;   *160*
But by and by comes back to Romeo,
Who had but newly entertained revenge,
And to't they go like lightning, for, ere I
Could draw to part them, was stout Tybalt slain;
And as he fell, did Romeo turn and fly.   *165*
This is the truth, or let Benvolio die.

LADY CAPULET   He is a kinsman to the Montague,
                   Affection makes him false, he speaks not true:
                   Some twenty of them fought in this black strife,
                   And all those twenty could but kill one life. *170*
                   I beg for justice, which thou, Prince, must give:
                   Romeo slew Tybalt, Romeo must not live.

PRINCE   Romeo slew him, he slew Mercutio;
                   Who now the price of his dear blood doth owe?

MONTAGUE   Not Romeo, Prince, he was Mercutio's friend;   *175*
                   His fault concludes but what the law should end,
                   The life of Tybalt.

PRINCE   And for that offence
                   Immediately we do exile him hence.
                   I have an interest in your hearts' proceeding:
                   My blood for your rude brawls doth lie a-bleeding; *180*
                   But I'll amerce you with so strong a fine
                   That you shall all repent the loss of mine.
                   I will be deaf to pleading and excuses,
                   Nor tears nor prayers shall purchase out abuses:
                   Therefore use none. Let Romeo hence in haste, *185*
                   Else, when he is found, that hour is his last.
                   Bear hence this body, and attend our will:
                   Mercy but murders, pardoning those that kill.

                                                    Exeunt

Paper 2, Levels 4–7 Answer Booklet

First Name_____

Last Name_____

School   _____

Write your answer in this booklet.

You may ask for more paper if you need it.

Write below the title of the play you are writing about and the task number you choose.

Title of Play_____

Task Number ☐

You may use this page to plan your answer.

Mark Scheme for Papers 1 and 2, 1998 Levels 4–7

[Blank page]

CONTENTS

General guidelines for markers   2

Question-specific guidance   4

EXEMPLAR RESPONSES AND PERFORMANCE CRITERIA

Paper 1, Sections A and B   7

Performance criteria for reading

     Question 1   17

     Question 2   31

     Question 3   45

Paper 1, Section C   47

Performance criteria for writing

     Question 4a   61

     Question 4b   77

     Question 4c   93

Additional guidance for Paper 2   94

Paper 2   95

Performance criteria for Understanding and Response

     Task 1   108

     Task 2   120

     Task 3   142

     Task 4   156

     Task 5   172

     Task 6   190

General guidelines for markers

Make sure you are very familiar with the question papers and, in the case of Paper 2, the set scenes from the Shakespeare plays.

Read the mark schemes through carefully, looking at the exemplar responses in conjunction with the performance criteria.

When you are marking follow the key points given opposite, with the performance criteria and exemplar responses for each question in front of you.

At the end of each question in Paper 1, write the level awarded for that question and then the mark, which should be circled, in the right-hand margin. At the end of each response to a Shakespeare task in Paper 2, write U/R (Understanding and Response) and W/E (Written Expression) both followed by a level and a mark which should be circled. **Any response which does not fulfil sufficient criteria to be awarded the lowest level available should be given a mark of O.**

Key points

- Mark Paper 1 and Paper 2 separately, question by question, referring regularly to the performance criteria and exemplar responses.

- As you look at each response decide which set of performance criteria best describes the performance.

- Look for evidence that the performance criteria have been fulfilled and judge your childs performance in each answer as a whole. Weaknesses in one area can be compensated for by strengths in another.

- Do not allow any part of the performance criteria to assume more importance than the rest and thereby become a hurdle.

- A response does not have to fulfil all the criteria in any level to be awarded that level.

- When you have decided which level the response falls into, judge whether it fulfils most of the criteria or whether it fulfils only some of the criteria; in other words, judge where in the level the response comes. Having decided this, read off the mark in the mark column and record it. **Use only the marks shown and not any intermediate ones.**

- **Keep looking for evidence of positive achievement and if you think a response is one level rather than another give it the full mark for that level. Avoid over use of borderline marks.**

Question-specific guidance

Paper 1: Reading *(Questions 1, 2 and 3)*

- These questions assess reading and not writing. Even if some of the answers are poorly expressed, pupils may show evidence of the positive achievement that is described in the performance criteria.

- Remember that different numbers of marks are allocated to different questions. Refer to the mark column in each set of performance criteria before awarding a mark.

- Answers to question 1 may be short but may still show enough understanding to gain 4, 5 or 6 marks.

Paper 1: Writing *(Questions 4a, b and c)*

- You should make a best-fit judgement about your child's responses in relation to the performance criteria, giving due consideration to the accuracy of the grammar, spelling, and punctuation.

- Do not be unduly influenced by the length of answers. Look for quality rather than quantity

- If an answer is only tenuously linked with the set topic, first decide which set of performance criteria most closely matches its qualities as a piece of writing, regardless of topic, to award a level. Then reduce the mark awarded to reflect the lack of relevance of the answer. Do not go below the next level down.

- If your child has written in a completely different genre from that required by the question, but has written on the set topic, apply the performance criteria as normal. Because the response will not fulfil the parts of the performance criteria which relate to form, the normal marking process will address this and no additional reduction in level needs to be made.

- Remember that your child completes this section at the end of the paper and may be running out of time. You must reward what is there, but you should take a lenient view of deteriorating handwriting.

- Your child may answer on more than one topic. In this case, mark both or all the pieces and award the level and mark gained by the best piece.

- Do not award marks other than those allowed by the mark scheme.

Paper 2

- Read and mark each answer twice, once for Understanding and Response and once for Written Expression.

- Pupils may score well for Understanding and Response, even though their Written Expression is weak, and vice versa. These are two separate assessments based on different criteria. Beware of falling into a pattern of automatically awarding the same level for Written Expression as for Understanding and Response.

- Some responses may not focus very closely on the question, but may, nevertheless, show understanding of the play. Reward any positive evidence of achievement, referring regularly to the performance criteria and examplar responses.

- Some responses may be largely narrative or include some paraphrasing of the text. However, before concluding that these are low-level responses, look for any evidence that the performance criteria at the higher levels have been met. For example, the selection of details and arrangement of ideas may show evidence of Understanding and Response which should be rewarded. Examples of how to reward such answers are given in the commentaries linked to the exemplar responses.

- If pupils have written in the third person in response to Tasks 2 or 4, use the criteria for Written Expression for Tasks 1, 5 or 6 rather than those specifically for empathetic responses. It is not necessary for your child to adopt any particular voice when writing about their ideas for directing the scene in Task 3.

- Do not award marks for Understanding and Response other than those allowed by the mark scheme.

Paper 1, Sections A and B

Question 1:	What impression do you get of the museum attendant's attitude towards snakes?	
Example	**Level exemplified**	**Page number**
1	below 4	8
2	4	9
3	5	10
4	6	11
5	7	12
6	above 7	14
Performance criteria for Question 1		17

Question 2:	How does the writer make you feel increasingly sorry for Miss Aitcheson?	
Example	**Level exemplified**	**Page number**
7	below 4-	18
8	4	19
9	5-	21
10	6	23
11	7	25
12	above 7	27
Performance criteria for Question 2		31

Question 3:	How does the leaflet try to change people's opinions about wolves?	
Example	**Level exemplified**	**Page number**
13	below 4-	32
14	4	33
15	5	35
16	6	37
17	7	39
18	above 7	42
Performance criteria for Question 3		45

Please note: answers to questions in Sections A and B of Paper 1 are marked for Reading and Understanding only. Written Expression, including grammar, punctuation, spelling and handwriting, is assessed in Section C of Paper 1.

QUESTION 1

Example 1

> the impression i get about the way the museum attendant tells about the snake is of it being harmless and a friendly snake. I think that the museum attendant sees his Job as a nice Job because in the story the attendant has a Nice attuide

Example 1

This answer contains a straightforward retelling of the museum attendant's repeated references to the snake being harmless and friendly. The comments about his seeing his job 'as a nice Job' and having a 'nice attuide' are imprecise and ambiguous. This answer, which makes a single point, only justifies a mark in the range below Level 4.

Key Consideration

- brief, simple retelling of what museum attendant says.

Level: below 4   Mark: 1

Other typical comments at this level might include:

- The museum attendant keeps saying snakes are harmless.
- He wants to teach the children about snakes.

Example 2

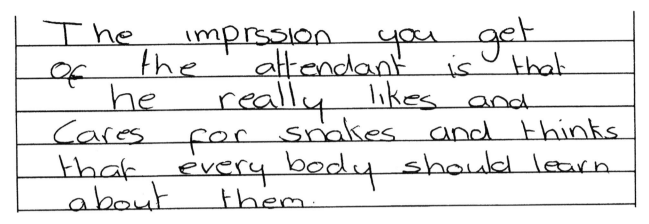

The imprssion you get
of the attendant is that
he really likes and
cares for snakes and thinks
that every body should learn
about them.

Example 2

This answer offers a brief explanation of the museum attendant's attitude – 'he really likes and cares for snakes' – and the way this affects his behaviour towards visitors – 'he ... thinks that every body should learn about them'. The comments are generalised and not supported by specific references to the text but nevertheless are clearly derived from it. Hence, a mark in the Level 4 range is justified.

Key Consideration

- brief explanation of museum attendant's attitude.

Level: 4   Mark: 2

Other typical comments at this level might include:

- The museum attendant sees the snakes as beautiful and harmless.
- The attendant enjoys working with snakes and tries to persuade people to like snakes.

Example 3

> The attendant seemed to like snakes he has
> been working with them for years. The attendant
> wanted the children to like the snake. The attendant
> thought you didn't have to be brave to
> be able to touch a snake they are harmless.
> In the attendants job he has to loves snakes.

Example 3

This pupil shows a general understanding of some aspects of the museum attendant's attitude: for example, he 'seemed to like snakes', thought 'they are harmless' and he wanted the children to share his views. The pupil picks up the point that the attendant had worked with snakes 'for years'. The implicit references to the text ('harmless', 'you didnt have to be brave') support the pupil's opinions, and although this is not a developed answer, there is enough explanation to place the answer in Level 5.

Key Considerations

- general understanding of museum attendant's attitude;
- implicit reference to what he says and does.

Level: 5   Mark: 3

Other typical comments at this level might include:

- The attendant is very protective towards the grass snake and keeps saying it is harmless.
- He tries to get the teacher and pupils to overcome their fear of snakes and treat them with respect.

Example 4

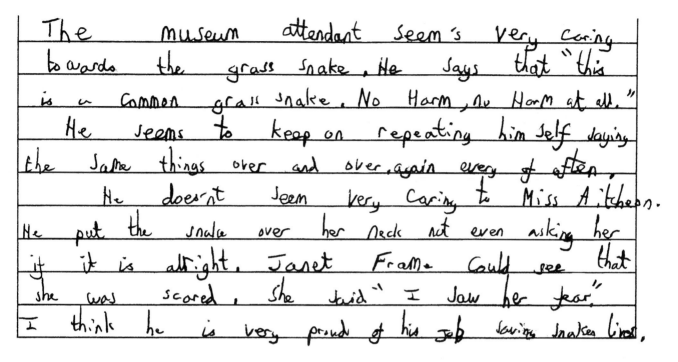

The museum attendant seem's very caring towards the grass snake. He says that "this is a common grass snake. No Harm, no Harm at all." He seems to keep on repeating him self saying the same things over and over again every of often. He doesn't seem very Caring to Miss Aitcheson. He put the snake over her neck not even asking her if it is alright. Janet Frame could see that she was scared, she said " I saw her fear." I think he is very proud of his job saving snakes lives.

Example 4

This pupil gives an explanation which begins to examine one or two aspects of the museum attendant's attitude in some detail. There is a comment that he seems 'very caring towards the grass snake' and that he is 'very proud of his job saving snakes lives' and this is supported by reference to the repetition of phrases like 'no Harm'. The implications of his commitment to snakes are explained in terms of its effect on his behaviour towards Miss Aitcheson – 'He does'nt seem very caring ... He put the snake over her neck not even asking ...'. This comment is linked to the text and supported by reference to Janet Frame, the writer, who recognises that 'she was scared ...'. Hence, this response is given a mark in the Level 6 range.

Key Considerations

- explains some aspects of museum attendant's attitude in detail;
- attempts to explore some attitudes implied by his behaviour.

Level: 6   Mark: 4

Other typical comments at this level might include:

- He picks up the snake as if it were an everyday object and seems to resent people being afraid of it.
- The attendant is anxious to persuade people that snakes should not be killed but loved.

Example 5

① The attendant feels a lot for the snakes and wants people to see them as gentle creatures - "No harm, no harm at all"

He wants people to be able to touch the snake like he can - "Now who else is going to be brave enough"

The attendant went to the snake before the teacher which shows he regards them highly - "picked up the snake and nursed it"

He obviously enjoys his job because he's been doing it for ~~years~~ a long time - "He'd been working with snakes for years"

He wants to help people in his job - "Teach the children to learn the feel of them".

He's very into his job and almost unaware of other things - "his perception had grown a reptilian covering"

Example 5

This pupil works through the text, drawing out evidence of the museum attendant's attitude and, initially, this may appear a straightforward answer consisting of brief comments supported by references. However, the individual comments – for example, 'The attendant went to the snake before the teacher', 'Teach the children to learn the feel of them'", 'almost unaware of other things' – are all directly relevant to the question and link together into a reasonably developed explanation, referring to the way the attendant's enthusiasm for snakes is reflected in his commitment to his job and his insensitivity to people. This response, therefore, is awarded a mark in the Level 7 range.

Key Considerations

- explores the implications of museum attendant's behaviour;
- comments well supported by textual reference.

Level: 7   Mark: 5

Other typical comments at this level might include:

- When the museum attendant says 'There is no need to be brave, it is not a question of bravery. The snake is harmless, absolutely harmless', he sounds as if he is mocking people's fears of snakes.
- He seems more concerned about the snake than about Miss Aitcheson when she throws it down because he picks it up and 'nurses' it.

Example 6

The Museum attendant is very sure of himself and
is not the slightest bit afraid of the snakes he has to
handle in his job. He talks about the snakes at ease
and in an informed way which would be helpful
if he wanted people to trust him and the snake.
The attendant sees his job as a way to get
through to people about how harmless and friendly
snakes can be. He takes his job seriously and is
brisk and methodical when he is working. This
can give him a cold and unfriendly air about
his attitude but he is just trying to make people
understand. about snakes. when he sayes.. "There is
no need to be brave, It's not a question of bravery.
The snake is harmless, absolutely harmless." He
sounds like he is mocking their fear and maybe
resenting them slightly for the fact they come from
the town.

Example 6

This response demonstrates a perceptive understanding of the museum attendant's attitude and gives a full account of the way he approaches his job, exploring the implications of much that he says and does. A combination of inferences and speculation referring to his character ('very sure of himself ... not the slightest bit afraid of the snakes'), motivation ('He takes his job seriously') and feelings ('He sounds like he is mocking their fear and maybe resenting them slightly') are based on a thoughtful, coherent response to the whole passage. This pupil shows insight into the way the museum attendant is portrayed and comments are clearly rooted in the text. Hence, a mark in the range above Level 7 is justified.

Key Considerations

- perceptive, detailed answer;
- insight into how attendant is portrayed.

Level: above 7   *Mark: 6*

Other typical comments at this level might include:

- The museum attendant is really mocking Miss Aitcheson's fear of snakes when he says 'Teacher is not afraid', and 'pronounces judgement on her' in a way that allows no escape.
- He handles the snakes confidently so everyone can see they're harmless.

Fold out this flap for the performance criteria for Question 1.

Q. No	Marks available	What impression do you get of the museum attendant's attitude towards snakes?
1	6	In your answer you should comment on: • the way the museum attendant talks about and handles the snake; • the way he sees his job.

Performance Criteria	Level	Mark
Pupils make one or two points about what the museum attendant says or does with reference to snakes though some misunderstanding may also be evident. They may simply retell what he does or says.	below 4	1
Pupils give a little explanation of some aspect of the museum attendant's attitude towards snakes, perhaps paraphrasing or making a generalised comment about what he says or does. They make simple references though they may tend simply to repeat what is in the text.	4	2
Pupils give an explanation of what the museum attendant says or does which shows a general understanding of one or two aspects of his attitude, though they do not develop any points in detail. They refer to one or two words or phrases to illustrate their opinions.	5	3
Pupils begin to explain in detail one or two aspects of the museum attendant's attitude, and their answers are generally rooted in the text or supported by appropriate references. They show an awareness of how his attitude is implicit in the way he handles the snake and deals with visitors to the museum, though they may not comment explicitly on these.	6	4
Pupils give a reasonably developed explanation that shows a clear understanding of the museum attendant's attitude, including some of the implications of the way he handles the snake and his treatment of visitors to the museum. Their comments are rooted in the text or supported by well-selected references.	7	5
Pupils give a perceptive answer which shows an appreciation of how the attendant is portrayed. Their comments are rooted in a coherent reading of the text or justified by well-selected references.	above 7	6

Question 1

Assessment Objectives

The question assesses pupils' ability to understand and respond to:

- the writer's presentation of character and situation;

- implied and explicit ideas.

> This is a short question with fewer marks available than questions 2 and 3. It is important to reward fully those answers that fulfil the criteria which may be comparatively brief but still show enough understanding to gain 4, 5 or 6 marks.

QUESTION 2

Example 7

> By saying how frightend she was ~~big~~ of the snake, by the way she was being laughed at and mocked.

Example 7

This very brief answer shows understanding of the basic situation Miss Aitcheson finds herself in; she was frightened of the snake and was laughed at. There is an implicit understanding in the choice of the word 'mocked' that these are valid reasons for feeling sorry for the teacher, but there is no attempt to make this explicit. Hence, Level 4 is not reached, but the pupil gains one mark for showing some understanding of what arouses our sympathy for Miss Aitcheson.

Key Consideration

- gives one reason for feeling sorry for Miss Aitcheson.

Level: below 4-   *Mark: 1*

Other typical comments at this level might include:

- Miss Aitcheson is old.
- She does not like the snake around her neck.
- The museum attendant just gives her the snake without asking.
- Some of the children laugh at her.

Example 8

2. The writer makes you feel sorry for miss Hitcheon by descrbeing her as a elderley teacher almost at retireng age.
When she is given the snake to hold she go's all rigid and appears to be holding her breath as if shes terricied

The museum attendant and the pupils seem to ignore the fact that she looks terrified.

Example 8

This pupil describes some of the ways sympathy for Miss Aitcheson is aroused: her age, her reactions to being given the snake to hold and the fact that her obvious discomfort is ignored. Hence, the answer is mainly factual and narrative with only the occasional implied comment. However, the selection of material offers relevant grounds for feeling sympathy for the teacher and merits a mark in the Level 4 range.

Key Considerations

- factual answer that offers relevant reasons for feeling sorry for Miss Aitcheson;
- beginning to make simple inferences but little comment.

Level: 4   *Mark: 4*

Other typical comments at this level might include:

- Miss Aitcheson is an elderly teacher who has not had much experience of snakes.
- When the snake moves, it really frightens her.
- She was forced to hold the snake because the children were there.
- She thought the pupils did not respect her any more.

Example 9

The writer makes me feel sorry for miss Aitcheson because she sounds terrified of snakes yet the attendant makes her hold a snake. The way miss Aitcheson reacts to having the snake around her neck is terrified you can tell this by the way the writer said that she froze when the snake was put on her. The museum attendant makes her hold the snake because he knows she is scared of snakes, but he is also doing it so the children can see there is nothing to be afraid of. The writers reaction to what happens is good, instead of standing around and embarassing the theather she leaves.

Example 9

This pupil gives an explanation of the main events which shows an understanding of the situation Miss Aitcheson is in. The pupil comments on how the teacher's fear is revealed through the writer's description of her response to having the snake placed round her neck, with an implied awareness of the attendant's insensitivity to her feelings in his anxiety to show the children 'there is nothing to be afraid of'. The pupil's statement that Miss Aitcheson 'froze when the snake was put on her' implicitly recognises the impact of '... stood rigid; she seemed to be holding her breath'. Hence, through the use of this limited but relevant selection of material, there is some recognition of how the reader is made to feel sorry for Miss Aitcheson, although these points are not developed and other aspects of the text are ignored. Some aspects of Level 5 performance are evident in a limited way and so this answer gains a mark in the Level 5 range.

Key Considerations

- some explanation of main events;
- implicit reference to language.

Level: 5-   Mark: 5

Other typical comments at this level might include:

- Miss Aitcheson 'stood rigid' and was 'holding her breath' which shows she was not enjoying the experience.
- She was very scared of holding the snake but has to hide this from her class.
- The attendant makes things worse for her by saying, 'She's not afraid of it at all'.
- The writer feels sorry for Miss Aitcheson and has to turn away.

Example 10

The writer stresses that anything the teacher does wrong is because of her up bringing. "it was not her fault, she was city-bred" The teacher is show as quite old and frail with a genuine fear of snakes, "elderly teacher" "never held a snake in her life". The writer gives the impression she is quite frail and scared again by describing her as pale and having to drag the fear from her eyes.

The teacher tenses up after having the snake on her and her fear is clearly shown. "she. lifted her hands in panic to get rid of the snake". ~~and~~ This makes you feel sorry but also gives you a sense she is quite brave at holding the snake

The attendant is forceful with the teacher which makes you feel emotional for ~~fear~~ her "before the teacher could protest, draped it round her neck". The children laughing at the teacher at the end also gives the impression she is being persecuted for her fear, "the children began to laugh". The writer at the end then tells us that none of the events are the teachers fault "she ... started to cry".

Example 10

This answer begins rather uncertainly but quickly focuses on how sympathy for Miss Aitcheson is generated by her age and upbringing. Her fears when the snake is placed round her neck causing her to tense up and the 'forceful' behaviour of the attendant are both referred to as further triggers for the reader's sympathy, leading to the climax of the children's laughter which 'gives the impression she [Miss Aitcheson] is being persecuted for her fear'.

Some aspects of the text are explored in some detail and the pupil selects quotations that both effectively support comments and also imply an awareness of their impact upon the reader.

All the performance criteria for Level 6 are evident, and so a mark in that range is awarded.

Key Considerations

- focus on ways in which sympathy is created for Miss Aitcheson;
- some aspects of the text explored in detail.

Level: 6   Mark: 8

Other typical comments at this level might include:

- Miss Aitcheson is described as 'near retiring age' and 'a city woman', so she would not have much experience of snakes.
- The writer makes you feel sorry for her because of the way the attendant puts the snake round her neck before she can refuse.
- We feel sorry for her because she is so brave at first, keeping up a front for the children, but then the snake moves and she can bear it no longer.
- The writer walks away because she cannot bear the way Miss Aitcheson was tortured by the whole thing.

Example 11

At the end of reading this passage we really feel sorry for Miss Aitcheson. This emotion is built up as we read and is started as soon as she is introduced.

"She must be near retiring age"

This makes us feel that she is old and weak, and makes us feel even more pityful as she gets distressed.

The writer also shows her obvious fear of the snake and we try to think how hard it must be for her to overcome this fear and actually hold the snake.

This is also accompanied by the fact that the attendant is oblivious to all this and we think he is being cruel to her as he constantly orders her not to be afraid. He also seems to drag the situation out as long as possible

"Miss Aitcheson can stand there with a beautiful snake around her neck, and touch it and stroke it and not be afraid.

He also keeps on urging her to speak to the children despite her fear and is very forceful that she should do so.

The final point that really makes us feel sorry is what happens at the end. She is smiling, just coming to terms with the snake when it darts for her and she screams. We think that it is sad that just as she started to like it, it reacts and reduces her to a sobbing wreck.

Example 11

The pupil begins with a general statement based on the requirements of the question and attempts to identify various points in the passage where sympathy is generated. Reference is made to Miss Aitcheson's fear, the attendant's insensitivity and the final effect of the snake's sudden movement. Some aspects of the text are commented on in detail; for example, the quotation 'She must be near retiring age' shows the pupil commenting quite perceptively on the impact of the writer's choice of language. There is a constant awareness of how the situation generates increasing sympathy for Miss Aitcheson: 'makes us feel even more pityful'; 'drag the situation out as long as possible'; 'keeps on urging her'; 'just coming to terms with the snake when it darts for her'; 'reduces her to a sobbing wreck'.

Initially this may appear a relatively brief answer that does not engage with the text in detail. Closer inspection, however, reveals a response that focuses clearly on the question, demonstrates how the reader's sympathies for Miss Aitcheson are increasingly aroused and justifies comments by textual reference. This response, therefore, merits a mark in the Level 7 range.

Key Considerations

- focus on ways in which sympathy is increasingly created for Miss Aitcheson;
- some aspects of the text explored in detail.

Level: 7   Mark: 10

Other typical comments at this level might include:

- Everything we are told about Miss Aitcheson at the start suggests she is vulnerable – 'near retiring age', 'a city woman', 'her face was pale'.
- The words 'defeat' and 'helplessness' make you realise how bad she feels and makes the reader sorry for her.
- The attendant makes the situation more tense by claiming she is not afraid when she is and no one knows what will happen next.
- We sympathise with her because eventually the combination of the attendant's attitude, fear of the snake and the need to stay calm in front of the children is too much for her.

Example 12

It all starts when it first becomes apparent that Miss Aicheson has a fear of snakes, it is obvious that she only wants to ~~watch what~~ observe. ~~It is then that the~~

"May I watch."

It is then that the attendant notices and begins to use it against her. He suggests that she should hold the snake first and gives a good reason that a teacher she could not refuse.

"The best way to get through to the children is to start with teacher."

Miss Aicheson has to do it in order to retain her respect from the children and her own pride.

The moment the snake is put around her neck she becomes petrified in this we know that she will not be able to stay like that for long.

"Miss Aicheson stood rigid, she seemed to be holding her breath."

From that point on it seems as if the attendant is enjoying the discomfort of Miss Aicheson and you begin to feel for her very much. He trys to prolong the ordeal for as long as possible. He always repeats the word 'afraid' refuring to Miss Aicheson even though he knows that she is.

"Teachers not afraid, are you?

He then, as if to make it worse, suggests that she handles the snake, it's as if he wants to break her, shatter her completely.

It is the end which moves you the most, it seems, to her, that the whole world is against her.

She drops the snake because she cannot stand the snake any longer and you can see that she is 'broke' and deeply ashamed.

"She collapsed into a small canvas chair and started to cry." As if to worsen the way she feels the attendant shows no sympathy towards her and is more interested in the well being of the snake.

Finally she tries to find comfort in her class but even they have no 'heart', the writer shows this by saying

"they were shut against her."

The only person who really seems to show some respect for her in the end is the writer as he ~~finally~~ does not wait any longer.

"I didn't feel I should wait any longer

Example 12

This answer immediately focuses on the way in which the reader is made to feel increasingly sorry for Miss Aitcheson. Initially, the pupil confuses the teacher with the narrator, suggesting that 'May I watch' implies a fear of snakes which the attendant registers and determines to use against her. He gives her the snake to hold because he knows as a teacher 'she could not refuse'. Miss Aitcheson becomes 'petrified' – 'Miss Aicheson stood rigid' – and the attendant 'trys to prolong the ordeal' repeating the word 'afraid'. The answer continues in this vein to track the increasing tension in the situation and to focus on the impact of significant words and phrases.

This is a full answer that shows an appreciation of some of the ways the writer creates increasing sympathy in the reader for Miss Aitcheson. References are well chosen and explored in a way that shows a perceptive response to some aspects of the writer's technique. The response justifies a mark in the range above Level 7.

Key Considerations

- reasonably full answer that shows awareness of the build-up of sympathy for Miss Aitcheson;
- detailed exploration of references showing understanding of the significance of the writer's choice of vocabulary.

Level: above 7   Mark: 11

Other typical comments at this level might include:

- 'Lurked like a dark stain' makes it clear from the start that this 'city woman' is ashamed of her fear of snakes and tries to suppress it to 'the depths'.
- The writer says, 'I could see her defeat and helplessness' which shows Miss Aitcheson is very frightened but for the sake of the children she whispers that she is not afraid.
- The writer has created sympathy for Miss Aitcheson because she makes the attendant appear very reasonable and the children admire their teacher but it is clear no one wants to touch the snake.
- She ends up collapsing in tears in front of everyone and is so humiliated by this 'useless torture' that the writer has to walk away.

Fold out this flap for the performance criteria for Question 2.

Q. No	Marks available	How does the writer make you feel increasingly sorry for Miss Aitcheson?
2	11	In your answer you should comment on: • the way Miss Aitcheson is described; • the way she reacts to having the snake around her neck; • the way the museum attendant and the children treat Miss Aitcheson; • the way the story ends and the writer's reaction to what happens.

Performance Criteria	Level	Mark
Pupils' answers are likely to be brief or almost entirely narrative. They make one or two points which show understanding of the main events or characters although some misunderstanding may also be evident.	below 4- below 4	1 2
Pupils' answers give a little explanation which shows an understanding of what happens to Miss Aitcheson. Their answers are largely factual and narrative but pupils are able to recognise some of the reasons why the reader feels sorry for Miss Aitcheson. Pupils' selection of facts is generally relevant to the question and they show some ability to refer to the text and make simple inferences.	4- 4	3 4
Pupils give an explanation of the main events, which shows a general understanding of the passage, relating most of their answer to the reader's sympathy for Miss Aitcheson. Their ideas are illustrated by references to the text or by the use of particular words or phrases which imply some awareness of the effects they create.	5- 5	5 6
Pupils give an answer which makes some attempt to show how the writer creates a feeling of sympathy for Miss Aitcheson. Ideas are supported by detailed comment on the significance of some parts of the text, although pupils may not deal equally with all aspects of the question. Their views are supported by appropriate references to the text that imply some awareness of the effects of the writer's use of language.	6- 6	7 8
Pupils give a reasonably full answer which comments on some of the ways in which the writer elicits sympathy for Miss Aitcheson and begins to discuss how this is built up in the passage. Their comments show an engagement with the text and are supported by well-selected references which demonstrate an awareness of the effect of the writer's use of language.	7- 7	9 10
Pupils give a full answer which shows an appreciation of how the writer achieves her effects. Their answers discuss how some aspects of the language and structure are used to make the reader feel increasingly sorry for Miss Aitcheson. Comments are justified by the skilful use of well-chosen references.	above 7	11

Question 2

Assessment Objectives

The question assesses pupils' ability to understand and respond to:

- the writer's presentation of character and situation;

- implied and explicit ideas;

- the writer's narrative technique, including use of language.

> **Pupils have a large quantity of relevant material available to choose from in answering this question. Do not expect them to cover everything; award marks for their selection of points in accordance with the performance criteria.**

Example 13

> The leaflet describes mene people repect to wolfs very hily and in one or two sentasis it sez lots of people have studied this species and hold wolves in deep respect.

Example 13

This brief answer paraphrases the point in the passage that some people 'hold wolves in deep respect'. Identification of this single point, which is central to the purpose of the leaflet, is worth a mark, but this answer fails to gain enough marks to be placed in the Level 4 range.

Key Consideration

- identification of one central point.

Level: below 4-   *Mark: 1*

Other typical comments at this level might include:

- The leaflet says that people are brought up to hate wolves.
- It says what wolves are really like.
- The leaflet shows pictures of friendly looking wolves.
- I think the leaflet could change people's minds about wolves.

Example 14

3) The leaflet tells us that the people who study wolfes know that they are respected, intelligent, devoted and skilled in hunting abilities

People fear and hate wolves because many of us were brought up to fear the villian in fairy tales and myths. There is also alot of competetion between man and wolf over food and land and the results of this has been a long one-sided battle, and this made the wolf the most misunderstood and persecuted animal. ~~The writer of the leaflet has picked out the go.~~

The writer of the leaflet has picked out the good details about the wolf eg. like how intelligent it is. It has also told us we hate the made up fairy tale villan.

The leaflet shown is very interesting and will succeed in changing peoples views about wolves and any wild dog.

Example 14

This answer is mainly descriptive, paraphrasing a number of points in the passage about wolves. There is an awareness of the contrast between the 'villian' portrayed in fairy tales and myths and 'how intelligent' the wolf is. A final sentence comments in a general way on the effect of the leaflet but the strength of this answer lies in its selection of relevant points supported by brief explanation. A mark in the Level 4 range is therefore awarded.

Key Considerations

- largely descriptive of the leaflet's contents;
- brief answer on relevant points.

Level: 4   *Mark: 4*

Other typical comments at this level might include:

- The leaflet says that people believe myths and fairy stories and hate wolves.
- The leaflet tries to persuade the reader by giving the true nature of wolves.
- This leaflet shows how wolves live in families and are kind to each other.
- It changes people's opinions of wolves because it gives you the real facts.

Example 15

They say things like people have feelings of hate towards the wolfs, from either Myth are fairy tale.

The leaflet is saying that most people hate the wolf and really there is no ~~need~~ need to hate them.

but Some of the people that have not gone on Myths and fairytales and have decided to go and study the species have become to have respect for them and they admire there way of life, and the intelligence which they have, so, the leaflet is saying don't Judge them by what other people say about wolfs.

The writer says that they are in some countrys on the brink of extinction so if you help them you could prevent that from happening in other countrys.

Some people think that wolfs just kill people but the fact of the point is that they don't just do that.

Wolfs are very intelligent creatures which shouldn't be underminded, and that is the point which the writer is trying to get a cross.

The pictures which have been put on the leaflet are trying to make the 'wolf look quite cute, and 'trying to make you want to help them.
I think that the wolf should be admired for its intelligence and not underminded for the fairy tales about it.
and this leaflet proberbly will make some people belive that to.

Example 15

This pupil's answer clearly covers the areas suggested in the prompts, giving an overview of the main points although it does so in a fairly superficial way. There is some reference to the text (for example, to people's perception of wolves being based on 'myth' and 'Fairy tale') to threats to their survival, and to wolves' intelligence. The pupil has evidently grasped the way in which the leaflet contrasts many people's impression of the wolf with the reality of how wolves live, and this contrast forms the basis of the pupil's often vague answer. This tends to mean that there is some repetition, for example, references to the wolf's 'intelligence', without looking further into the way the leaflet builds on this contrast to persuade the reader. The pupil has identified one of the purposes behind the use of the pictures, which are 'trying to make the wolf look cute', and sees that this will encourage people to help wolves. There is also evidence of implicit understanding of the use of the section 'How you can help' in persuading people to help prevent the extinction of wolves. The pupil's answer has been awarded a mark in the Level 5 range.

Key Considerations

- gives an overview of the ideas in the leaflet;
- demonstrates general, sometimes undeveloped understanding of how the leaflet tries to persuade.

Level: 5   Mark: 6

Other typical comments at this level might include:

- The leaflet explains why people have no reason to hate wolves and threaten their survival.
- Wolves live in families and are 'friendly and loyal' and are related to dogs.
- The pictures of the wolves show them in a more attractive light and make them look appealing/ friendly.
- My opinion started to change when I read of their intelligence and devotion to their family.

Example 16

Many people think of wolves as the type in the fairy tales where they killed and ate people, many people fear them. Yet, if you study wolves you will see that wolves are intelligent and friendly. The leaflet tries to change people's opinions about wolves by explaining the above. They have put photos of wolves looking innocent and of a family of wolves onto the leaflet. This immediately changes your opinion towards them as they look very different to what many people have put into their minds. The wolf facts that have been used on the leaflet tell you what food they really eat and how to our surprise they actually eat berries. The leaflet also has a section on family life this tells us how they live, how they enjoy playing together, the friendship, loyalty and need in their packs. Pups are the focal point for the whole family with uncles and aunts all helping to provide food and care. Intelligent and friendly, the wolf is one of nature's

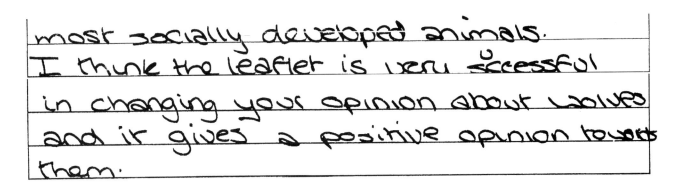

most socially developed animals.
I think the leaflet is very successful
in changing your opinion about wolves
and it gives a positive opinion towards
them.

Example 16

This pupil begins with a summative comment on the contrast between popular misconceptions of the wolf and the leaflet's intention to change these. The answer then goes on to explore some of the ways in which the leaflet attempts to achieve its effects, with comment on the pictures, the 'wolf facts', the significance of details of what wolves eat and the emphasis on the quality of their 'family life'. Comments are thoroughly rooted in the text, some aspects of which are explained in detail, with a clear focus on how each part contributes to the persuasive effect. If the comments on language and layout had been less descriptive and more analytical, then a Level 7 mark would have been justified, but this answer clearly merits a mark within the Level 6 range.

Key Considerations

- explores some aspects of the leaflet in detail;
- lacks precise comment on structure and choice of language.

Level: 6   Mark: 8

Other typical comments at this level might include:

- None of the wolves is showing its teeth, which is how we think of the wolf in 'Little Red Riding Hood'.
- The leaflet makes wolves sound almost human by showing a picture of a 'family portrait' and describing them as living in a 'family group'.
- Most words are used to create a positive image of wolves as 'intelligent', 'friendly' and 'socially developed' animals.
- This leaflet will make people feel sorry for wolves and want to do something.

Example 17

3. The leaflet entitled "The Wolf" tries to change people's minds about wolves.

Many people are very scared of wolves and this is because of the image that many stories give. The article actually tells you this when it says "in many people's subconsious is the "fictional" wolf - the villian of myth and fairy tale. In some ways it is the same idea as the snake and miss mitcheson but I do not think that many people would go and kill a wolf if they saw one, although many people fear wolves because of their bad reputation.

An example of this is when the wolf has to battle man for food to keep alive the wolf is always the nasty animal and "one of natures most misunderstood and persecuted animals."

The way in which the writer has set this article out would make you want to read it. For example, the pictures that are shown make the animal look very sweet with their ears pricked up and their big eyes looking right at you. I think the way in which the writer has put two small boxes in the article were good because your attention would immediatly be attracted to the larger front size as the headings "threats to survival" and "Wolf facts."

The information which has been selected by the writer would make quite a lot of people change their views about wolves. Lots of people who would read this have dogs and since the "domestic dogs are decensed from wolves" I think that lots of people would be more caring towards wolves. Most people will see the wolf as a monster but they will be encouraged to know that the animal feeds on "small rodents and berries."

The words in which the writer uses to express the positive side of wolves is that they are very intelligent and are good at hunting. One of the biggest threats to wolves becoming extinct is man. The other large point is the fact that if forests keep being demolished then the wolves will have no where to live.

You may think that the wolf is viscous but the one thing that keeps the "pack" together is "need, loyalty and friendship."

If, on the television you saw two wolves fighting you may think that if they can kill their own species they will kill anything. This is not the case because the animals are probably play fighting.

The animal is very clever in some actions that occure in its everyday life but some of these things are often mixed up with fear or hate of the animal.

I think that the article will succeed in the persuation of peoples views because it covers many aspects of the animal, who it's threat are and it's love toward the animals friends. I think many people will change their views, although they may still be scared of them. But I think this because mankind has always been frightened of the unknown and things which they do not know about even when there is no need to be.

Example 17

This answer is closely linked to the text and shows a clear understanding of how the leaflet attempts to persuade. Appropriate references such as '"need, loyalty and friendship"' and 'they will be encouraged to know that the animal feeds on "small rodents and berries"' show the pupil can recognise persuasive language and comment on it effectively. There are comments on the effects of the use of pictures and the structure of the leaflet, and an overall awareness that the information given has been selected deliberately. The answer concludes with a summative judgement on the overall impact of the leaflet and, despite not always maintaining its clear focus on the question throughout, demonstrates aspects of performance at Level 7. It is therefore awarded a mark in the Level 7 range.

Key Considerations

- reasonably developed answer closely linked to text;
- comments on various aspects of how the leaflet achieves its effects.

Level: 7   *Mark: 10*

Other typical comments at this level might include:

- The leaflet creates sympathy for wolves by claiming to give the 'truth' about them instead of our fears and prejudices.
- The writer selects information about 'family life' and 'threats to survival' with attractive pictures to persuade readers to change their minds.
- The wolf is described as 'on the brink of extinction' which makes us feel sorry for it, especially when we see the picture of it underneath looking intelligent and appealing.
- It might not change people's opinions because the leaflet is biased and people have had a stereotypical view of a wolf since childhood.

Example 18

3) How does the leaflet try to change peoples opinions about wolves?

The leaflet says that some people have "feelings of fear and hate" about wolves, but then goes on to say that people who have studied wolves actually have feelings of "deep respect" for these animals. It is saying that when most people think of wolves they think of the "fictional" wolf" and if they knew what wolves were really like they would admire them not hate them.

The writer selects information that gives a good view of wolves, saying that they live in "a tightly-knit family group" - where the term "family" is usually applied to humans. They mention that "all domestic dogs are descended from wolves". As most people like dogs this information might encourage them to like wolves too. As this information makes people like wolves, after it is information about how wolves can be saved, this is a sensible place to put it

Words such as "friendship, loyalty and need" are used to create a positive image of wolves. Again, these descriptions are more often used on humans as it makes people think wolves are more like humans. There is a lot of description of the animals communication abilitys, which makes them seem much more intelligent.

I think that this leaflet will be successfull to some readers, and the pictures also help a lot. They show the wolves looking harmless and more like dogs — this would probably change some dog-owners ~~opinion~~ opinions about wolves. The description of the wolf's family life is also very effective at changing peoples opinions, but there will always be some people who hate wolves so much that they will ignore this leaflet as soon as they read the title.

Example 18

The pupil demonstrates a perceptive understanding of the way in which the leaflet aims to persuade. The first paragraph summarises the main premise of the leaflet, and the pupil goes on to analyse the ways language, layout and structure are used. The pupil shows understanding of the section 'Family life' and provides a confident analysis of the strategies used by the leaflet: 'the term "family" is usually applied to humans'; 'Words such as "friendship, loyalty and need" are used to create a positive image of wolves'; 'it makes people think wolves are more like humans'. The pupil also anticipates the impact of the leaflet on dog-owners, saying that the pictures 'show the wolves looking harmless and more like dogs'. Also perceptive is the pupil's reference to the positioning of the section giving information about saving the wolf. The level of textual reference and analysis of language place this answer above Level 7.

Key Considerations

- analytical approach;
- skilful use of textual reference.

Level: above 7   *Mark: 11*

Other typical comments at this level might include:

- People's feelings are made to seem unreal because they come from myths and fairy tales, made up stories contrasted with the 'facts' which this leaflet provides.
- Words like 'threats to survival', 'persecuted' and 'habitat destruction' are intended to make us feel sorry for the wolf and guilty about our treatment of it.
- After all the good things it has said about them, the leaflet makes a final appeal by suggesting the wolves' situation is 'desperate', they 'deserve' a chance to survive and that 'Operation Wolf' is a major crusade.
- The leaflet could change people's opinions because it uses key elements – pictures, facts, good presentation and colour.

Fold out this flap for the performance criteria for Question 3.

Q. No	Marks available	How does the leaflet try to change people's opinions about wolves?
3	11	In your answer you should comment on: • how the leaflet describes many people's feelings about wolves; • how the writer has selected information about wolves to persuade the reader; • the way words and layout are used to try to create a positive image of wolves; • whether you think the leaflet will succeed in changing people's opinions about wolves.

Performance Criteria	Level	Mark
Pupils mention one or two of the main facts about wolves which might change the reader's opinion. They recognise that the leaflet is trying to persuade. There may be little or no reference to the text.	below 4-	1
	below 4	2
Pupils' answers are largely descriptive. They refer broadly to the ways the leaflet tries to persuade, selecting one or two relevant details and giving a little explanation. They refer to the text but do not link their comments to their references.	4-	3
	4	4
Pupils give an overview of the information and ideas in the leaflet though this may not always be closely linked to the text. They select some relevant points about wolves and describe their effect. They illustrate their comments by identifying some specific words, phrases or aspects of layout and explaining briefly how these might persuade the reader.	5-	5
	5	6
Pupils show some ability to explore how the leaflet aims to persuade the reader. They develop some of their points in detail, though they may not deal equally with all aspects of the question. Their comments on the persuasive techniques of the leaflet are supported by some appropriate references to its language and layout.	6-	7
	6	8
Pupils give a reasonably full answer which is closely linked to the text and shows an understanding of the ways the leaflet attempts to persuade the reader. The pupils develop ideas and comment in some detail on the effects of the leaflet's choice of language and the use of layout. They select appropriate references to support their points.	7-	9
	7	10
Pupils give a full answer which analyses the text and shows appreciation of the leaflet's persuasive qualities. They use textual references skilfully to justify their views by discussing how language, layout and structure are used to achieve specific effects.	above 7	11

Question 3

Assessment Objectives

The question assesses pupils' ability to understand and respond to:

- the information in the leaflet;

- the leaflet's purpose;

- how the ideas are presented, including the effects of language and layout;

- the overall impact of the leaflet.

> **Do not expect pupils to cover everything in the leaflet; award marks for their selection of points in accordance with the performance criteria.**

Paper 1, Section C

Question 4a: *Write a letter to headteachers of schools in the area encouraging them to bring groups of pupils to visit the museum.*

Question 4b: *Write about a frightening encounter with an animal.*

Question 4c: *Imagine you have been given a chance to talk in a year assembly. Choose an issue you feel strongly about. (It does not need to be about animals.)*

Example	Level exemplified	Page number
19 (4a)	below 4-	48
20 (4a)	4-	50
21 (4a)	5	52
22 (4a)	6	54
23 (4a)	7	56
24 (4a)	above 7	58
Performance criteria for Question 4a		61
25 (4b)	fails to meet mark scheme criteria	62
26 (4b)	4-	63
27 (4b)	5	65
28 (4b)	6	68
29 (4b)	7	71
30 (4b)	above 7-	73
Performance criteria for Question 4b		77
31 (4c)	below 4-	78
32 (4c)	4-	80
33 (4c)	5+	82
34 (4c)	6	85
35 (4c)	7	87
36 (4c)	above 7	89
Performance criteria for Question 4c		93

Please note: unless otherwise indicated in the commentary, all the exemplar letters were headed with an appropriate address and signed at the end. Such identifying marks have been removed to preserve the anonymity of the pupils concerned.

QUESTION 4a

Example 19

Dear Headteacher

At the PRIME MUSEUM
We will be having a special
Opening with a famous star with an
Exibit on the Victorian culture using
computar and live preformences.
And school the come get a 20%
discount. With the telephone number
at the top or Address confirm trip
by opening 9th Mayo

Your Sincerely

Example 19

Communication of ideas and impact on reader

This response is recognisably set out as a letter and some of the pupil's ideas are clearly expressed. However, apart from the initial appeal of 'a special opening with a famous star', there is little relevant information about the museum itself and the information about organising a visit is quite confused.

Structure and accuracy, including grammar, spelling and punctuation

The opening sentence is a little clumsy, but complex and just about secure grammatically, but otherwise control of sentence structure and sentence punctuation is weak. The spelling of simple and common polysyllabic words, for example, 'opening' and 'Victorian', is generally accurate, and handwriting is clear and legible.

Overall comment

This is a limited response to the task, but the pupil has produced a recognisable letter with an appropriate address and ending. Some information is clearly expressed and the spelling of the range of vocabulary employed is generally accurate. The response does not demonstrate aspects of performance at Level 4 and, on a 'best-fit' basis gains a mark in the range below Level 4.

Key Considerations

- some features appropriate to a letter;
- limited response, not always clearly expressed.

Level: below 4-   Mark: 2

Example 20

This pupil has written on topic a.

Dear Headteacher

the long awaited opening of the wild things museum is finely here.

after two years of building and Indepth reserch we are proud to bring you the most upto date museum of the liveing thing in the world.

the museum includes an aquaram, petting corner, life size modles working displays and education center, computers full of information and disabled facilitys and many maagh more educationa equiptments and fun things to do.

we are now offering you as an opening offer a half price class Ticket.

pleas contact me as soon as possible.

yours sincerely

Example 20

Communication of ideas and impact on reader

The pupil's answer is organised into paragraphs, and is in letter form. The letter is written in an appropriate and persuasive tone, with phrases such as 'long awaited', 'disabled facilitys' and 'we are now offering you' demonstrating the pupil's awareness of the kind of language required. However, the content is largely descriptive, and does not give any details about how to organise a trip to the museum.

Structure and accuracy, including grammar, spelling and punctuation

Whilst the pupil can demonstrate some ability to construct complex sentences ('the long awaited opening of the wild things museum is finely here' and 'after two years of building and indepth reserch we are proud to bring you'), capital letters are used only at the start of the letter and even in the address their use was sporadic. Spelling of simple words is generally accurate, although some familiar words are not correctly spelt ('pleas', 'modles') and there is evidence that the pupil has not mastered some common spelling patterns ('liveing', 'facilitys'). Handwriting is clear and legible.

Overall comment

Meaning is clearly conveyed in this letter through the use of some appropriate vocabulary, and sentences are accurately demarcated with full stops although capital letters are omitted. Applying the 'best-fit' principle, this answer merits a mark at the bottom of the Level 4 range.

Key Considerations

- an attempt at adopting an appropriate tone;
- weak punctuation and spelling.

Level: 4-   Mark: 8

Example 21

This pupil has written on topic a.

Dear Headteacher,

My name is Lisa Price
I am a directer of a new museum
which is opening next Saturday in the
city centre of Birmingham. I would
like to know wheather one of your
year groups would like to come and
vist my Museum. It is called Future Gallary.
It is a very young museum and is
suitible for ages 12-18. Inside there
will be games, quizzes and mental
tasks for the children to do. It is also
an educational day out too. There is
a cafe on the top floor and there
is a beutiful view all around. The
children will learn about the future
and what it has to offer the
cost of this trip is just £3.50
and if you would like your coach trip
included it will be just £5.00 for adults
and £4.50 for children. Parents are
welcome. We only have 60 places and the
children will be spilt up into 6 groups of

> 10 each group will have one of our tour guides as it is quite a large museum.
> If ~~a~~ you are interested.
> Please contact me on the number below
> Your Sincerly

Example 21

Communication of ideas and impact on reader

This piece is clearly structured and has a generally appropriate tone. The information given is straightforward but thoughtful and attempts to engage the reader by the use of appropriate detail and clear descriptions of the attractions of the museum: for example, 'games, quizzes and mental tasks'. The vocabulary is comparatively limited in range but appropriate ('suitible for ages', 'tasks for the children', 'educational day out') and some enticement is offered in terms of the price: 'just £3.50'.

Structure and accuracy, including grammar, spelling and punctuation

The letter is written in one main paragraph, but it is clear to read. Links between sentences are rather simple ('It is', 'There is') but a limited range of punctuation is generally used accurately. Spelling of simple words is usually correct, although 'directer', 'wheather' and 'beutiful' show there is a less secure grasp of polysyllabic words. Handwriting is generally clear and legible.

Overall comment

This is a relatively unsophisticated piece of writing but it is carefully and thoughtfully structured with an appropriate form and tone for a persuasive letter. It merits the award of a mark in the middle of the Level 5 range.

Key Considerations

- information generally clearly expressed in an appropriate tone;
- limited range of vocabulary and sentence structures.

Level: 5   Mark: 16

Example 22

This pupil has written on topic a.

Dear Headteacher

I am writing to you today on account of the new museum that is being built in our towns centre. I am to become the director of the museum and would like to invite you to bring groups of pupils along to my museum on an educational visit. The museum is a national history museum and the exhibits will include life size skeletons of dinosaurs and other creatures including an exhibit on the future world.

In the exhibits there will be many computers where the children can press a button and be swamped with information, pictures and small games to play. I have heard that as part of your KS2 syllabus at the moment your doing about transport and how it has improved over the years. Well there is a rather large exhibit based on the old factory, we have taught next door about that very thing. There is a life size model of Stevensons rocket and M/T fords first motorcar. The young children can see different models of trains in chronological order of what year they were built in and many other things. You can ~~imagine~~ organise a trip by ringing . and we will send your a special schools pack with a video and information on the museum. We can offer you special school offers with reduced

54

pupil prices and the teachers can come in free. We
hope to see you soon.

                        Yours Sincerely

Example 22

Communication of ideas and impact on reader

This is a well-organised and expressed letter with engaging ideas. The tone is appropriate and effective ('would like to invite', 'as part of your KS2 syllabus') and the specific details ('include life size skeletons of dinosaurs', 'life size model of Stevensons rocket') help make the letter persuasive as well as interesting. Vocabulary is varied and mature.

Structure and accuracy, including grammar, spelling and punctuation

There is some awareness of paragraphing, but this is not employed effectively although the information is organised in a logical way. Similarly, an ambitious attempt is made to use a range of simple and complex sentences but these are not always successfully managed. Punctuation is generally used accurately and spelling is correct, including some difficult words such as 'chronological'. Handwriting is in a fluent and legible style.

Overall comment

This letter is not headed with an address but otherwise uses a clear and appropriate form for an informative letter. The result is an engaging and persuasive piece with some unevenness and so a mark in the middle of the Level 6 range has been awarded.

Key Considerations

- clear and appropriate form;
- persuasively written with few inaccuracies.

                                        Level: 6   *Mark: 22*

Example 23

This pupil has written on topic a.

Dear Head teacher.

As The museum of science has just opened, we would like to welcome your school to visit us. We are sure here at the museum of science that are excibitions and excibits would be enjoyable and educational for your pupils.

One of the areas we believe that children will enjoy is the 'ANIMAL LAB.' This contains various displays and activities to help teach children about different animals. There is a special area in there about the most unusual animals in the world. There is also a 'feeley centre' where children put their hands in small boxes and feel different animals furs ie feathers, porcupine spikes ect.

We also have a video room, where we shows diffent video about many different aspects of science.

One of the ways children can learn is the fact that there are many practical excperaments which they can take part in, alone or with a supervisor.

We find children always enjoy spending money so we have a gift shop full of fun and interesting trinkets at a cheap price.

To encourage you and your school to visit the museum of science we offer a discount for school parties. We can arrange bookings and also a choice of videos in the video room in advance. ~~If you won~~

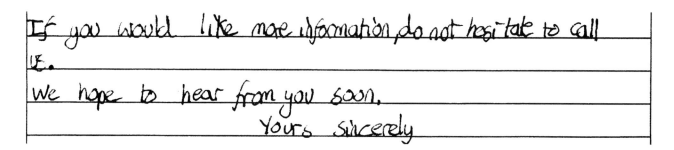

If you would like more information, do not hesitate to call
us.

We hope to hear from you soon.

Yours sincerely

Example 23

Communication of ideas and impact on reader

This response is written in a confident style. It has a polite and friendly tone – sustained by the use of the first and second person pronouns and the active voice– and is informative without being excessively formal. Details of the museum's facilities are described in a way that is persuasive– 'most unusual animals'; 'a 'feeley centre' '; 'video room'– in that it keeps the interests of children in mind. The choice of vocabulary is appropriate to tone and content – for example, 'supervisor', 'trinkets', 'discount' – and meaning is immediately clear. Instructions for organising a trip are brief but encouraging. All aspects of the task have been addressed effectively.

Structure and accuracy, including grammar, spelling and punctuation

Ideas are clearly presented in a structured way, supported by appropriate use of paragraphing. A range of simple and complex sentence structures is employed to good effect; in the final paragraph, for example, 'To encourage you and your school ...' gives a clear emphasis to the museum's support followed by 'We can arrange ...' and is concluded by a polite invitation: 'If you would like ...'. Sentences are accurately demarcated, although there is little use of internal sentence punctuation. Spelling is accurate except for 'exibitions', 'exibits', 'ect' and 'experments'. Handwriting is in a fluent and legible style.

Overall comment

This is a confident, well-structured letter that keeps purpose and audience firmly in mind and achieves an informative and friendly tone without strain. Sentence structures are varied and vocabulary is effectively used to make meaning clear. The piece is therefore worth a mark in the middle of the Level 7 range.

Key Considerations

- confidently written and organised;
- clear sense of purpose and audience;
- information presented persuasively through a range of grammatical devices.

Level: 7　　　*Mark: 28*

Example 24

This pupil has written on topic a.

Dear Headteacher,

I am writing to give you information about our new museum which will be opening soon. We wish to aid you, the teaching community, in teaching children about the history of the Human Race. We regulate our displays so that they are closely in line with the National Curriculum and will give useful and essential information to children in a way that could not be done in a classroom.

Some teaching materials are provided free of charge to aid the learning capacity of a day trip. Follow-up classroom exercises can also be obtained. Alongside many of the displays there are activity centres which are designed to give children a memorable and exciting, but also an educational day.

Our museum concentrates mainly on the history of Britain and British interaction with other countries in the past, but some displays look at American, African and Asian civilisations. During a day at our museum children will learn about what happened in the past. With some of these events activity rooms have been set up to mirror the events as they happen. For instance, what was it like to be in a French castle under siege from King Henry V and the English army? Or how did sailors feel at the Battle of Trafalgar? What was it like to be bombed during the Blitz? All these and many more are shown at our museum.

Children will also learn why the events are important. We can explain to them why the Norman Invasion is important, although it happened over 900 years ago. We will show that decisions taken hundreds of years ago are still important today, and

That knowledge of them is essential to living in today's world.

With Government funding we can offer exceptional prices and a practical education that could never be achieved in the classroom. We believe that seeing is not believing, but that hands-on experience is the best way to teach. We can interest the most uninterested pupil, educate those who have least capacity for learning by means of an exciting and memorable day out.

History made exciting at the Museum of Human History, London. We hope you will be interested and arrange a visit that could enhance the education of your pupils

Yours Sincerely

That knowledge of them is essential to living in today's world.

59

Example 24

Communication of ideas and impact on reader

This pupil manages to produce a letter of exceptional expression and organisation. Its tone is confident, mature and effective: 'We wish to aid you, the teaching community'; 'Follow-up classroom exercises can also be obtained'. The presentation of ideas and information through precise vocabulary ('We regulate our displays ... closely in line with the National Curriculum'; 'activity rooms have been set up to mirror the events') and specific detail ('what was it like to be in a French castle under siege ...') add to the success of the piece. All aspects of the task have been excellently addressed.

Structure and accuracy, including grammar, spelling and punctuation

The sophisticated grammatical structures ('With Government funding we can offer ...'; 'We believe that seeing is not believing, but that hands-on experience ...'), the controlled paragraphing and the faultless spelling produce a confident and coherent piece.

Overall comment

This exceptionally confident letter addresses its audience effectively and engagingly. The detailed material used and the sustained organisational skills displayed indicate the top mark is fully deserved.

Key Considerations

- coherent, persuasive and informative letter;
- good technical control of language.

Level: above 7+   *Mark: 33*

Fold out this flap for the performance criteria for Question 4a.

Q. No 4a	Imagine you are a director of a new museum. (You can decide what is in the museum.)
	Write a letter to headteachers of schools in the area encouraging them to bring groups of pupils to visit the museum.
Marks available	Write an address for the museum at the top. Begin your letter *Dear Headteacher* and end it with *Yours faithfully* and your signature.
33	In your letter you could write about: • what the museum has to offer; • why it is of educational value; • why young people will enjoy a visit and learn from it; • how to organise a trip there.

Performance Criteria	Level	Mark
Some of the pupils' ideas are clearly expressed and their writing shows some features which are appropriate to an informative letter. The basic grammatical structure of some sentences is correct and some punctuation is used accurately. The spelling of simple words is usually accurate and the handwriting is mostly legible, though there may be obvious weaknesses in the formation of some letters.	- below 4 +	2 4 6
The pupils' ideas are generally clear and mostly organised in an appropriate form for an informative letter. Sentence structures and vocabulary are beginning to be used to create an appropriate tone, although this may not be maintained. Punctuation to mark sentences is mostly used accurately and pupils are beginning to use punctuation within the sentence. The spelling of simple and common polysyllabic words is generally accurate. Handwriting is mostly clear and legible.	- 4 +	8 10 12
The pupils' writing is clearly expressed and the points are organised in an appropriate form for an informative letter, usually with a clear structure or paragraphs. Pupils try to engage and persuade the reader by such means as describing the facilities in the museum. The choice of vocabulary and sentence structures contributes to an appropriate tone, although this may not be maintained. A range of punctuation, including commas and apostrophes, is usually used accurately. Spelling, including that of words with complex regular patterns, is usually accurate. Handwriting is generally clear and legible in a fluent style.	- 5 +	14 16 18
Pupils use a clear and appropriate form for an informative letter and their writing is engaging and persuasive in parts. A varied vocabulary, a range of simple and complex sentences and appropriate paragraphing contribute to an effective tone for the writing, though the same quality may not be evident throughout. A range of punctuation is usually used correctly to clarify meaning. Spelling is accurate though there may be some errors in difficult words. Handwriting is in a fluent and legible style.	- 6 +	20 22 24
The pupils' writing is confident, organised and written in an appropriate tone, style and form for a letter presenting information. Although some of the ideas may be unsophisticated, they are linked and developed persuasively by a range of grammatical features and the effective use of vocabulary. Paragraphing and correct punctuation are used to make the sequence of points clear. Spelling, including that of complex irregular words, is correct. Handwriting is in a fluent and legible style.	- 7 +	26 28 30
The pupils' writing seeks to engage and persuade the reader by presenting information clearly and persuasively in a coherent way. The choice of style and structure, supported by the precise use of a range of vocabulary and grammatical structures, enables clarity and emphasis to be achieved. Pupils show a consistent grasp of the correct use of paragraphing and a range of punctuation. Spelling, including that of complex irregular words, is correct. Handwriting is in a fluent and legible style.	- above 7 +	31 32 33

QUESTION 4a

Assessment Objectives

This question assesses pupils' ability to:

- communicate ideas to a reader;

- use an appropriate style and tone;

- organise their writing appropriately for their chosen form;

- shape and structure their work using paragraphs, grammatical structures and punctuation to convey their meaning;

- choose words precisely and imaginatively and to spell them correctly;

- write clearly and legibly.

> **Pupils may not write at length for this option and so it is important to reward fully the qualities of a succinct but effective response. They are likely to demonstrate the quality of their writing through an appropriate choice of style, tone and vocabulary.**
>
> **Although pupils have been asked to write an address for the museum and should do so, if they do not provide an address this should not automatically prevent them from gaining any particular level. The absence of an address should be taken into consideration when assessing other aspects of form.**
>
> **Keep looking for evidence of positive achievement and if you think a response clearly deserves a particular level, place it securely in that level.**

Reminder

Use the performance criteria opposite in conjunction with the exemplar responses to assess the qualities of an answer on a 'best-fit' basis. You should make a judgement of the overall qualities of the response. Weaknesses in one area can be compensated for by strengths in another.

Please refer to page 8 of this mark scheme for guidance on marking the work of pupils who have used an amanuensis or a mechanical aid such as a word processor.

Example 25

> It was summer and I was on my bike, I was riding down the mountain, when I sore a moving animal, I jump off my bike and I went over to have a look and I sore a wolf. Then I looked away but the wolf was lookeding at me. Then I run away and the wolf run with me but I new I darent. He wasn't frightening me he wanted to play with me.

Example 25

Communication of ideas and impact on reader

This short response has a recognisably narrative opening, establishing season, place and circumstances with a straightforward, anecdotal tone. However, although some ideas are clearly expressed, there is no real development of plot other than the writer meeting a wolf, and the piece ends indeterminately.

Structure and accuracy, including grammar, spelling and punctuation

Sentences are usually correctly constructed, but this is undermined by a tendency to use commas instead of full stops as sentence markers. A range of vocabulary is used, but weaknesses in spelling simple words ('when I sore a moving animal'; 'I sore a wolf') make it difficult to understand the meaning. Handwriting is mostly clear and legible.

Overall comment

This is a very limited response to the task, with some features appropriate to a story. However, the weaknesses in the control of the language put it below the standards expected even in the below Level 4 range. In circumstances such as this the piece should be given a mark of 0.

Key Considerations

- very short response;
- some features appropriate to a simple narrative;
- very limited control of language;
- fails to meet mark scheme criteria.

Mark: 0

Example 26

This pupil has written on topic b.

I was walking in the woods
on a warm summers night when I
heared some noreing. I did not think
eny thing of it. I begem to get the
feeling that I was being foloved so
I turned on to a different path but
I still had the feeling that I was
being whatched. So I turned and
looked but there was nothing there
So I walked on. Then I heard some
growling So I sarted to run. I
looked back and then I saw them,
a pack of wild dogs they started
to run at me So I jumped
off the path they sarted to chase
me down So I ran down on to
the next path. and down on to
the one below. I thought I heved
lost them but there they were
behined to me So I ran straight-
on down the path they were
starting to get cloes So I jumped
the style. But they still cept coming
So I ran down on to the Scrubs
land and down in to the village they

63

hand stoped chaseing. I did not
tell eny one becames how would
be leull me. But I never Went
in to the woods by my self again.

Example 26

Communication of ideas and impact on reader

This is a straightforward piece of narrative with a clear opening and a satisfactory conclusion and an attempt to engage the reader's interest by suggesting suspense and mystery. Although events are clearly narrated, there is no real attempt to use effective descriptive words apart from 'a warm summers night' and the vocabulary is rather limited.

Structure and accuracy, including grammar, spelling and punctuation

Some of the words are hard to decipher ('noreing') and there are spelling errors in common words ('eny', 'chaseing'). The sequence of events is linked by using 'and', 'but' and 'so' repeatedly, but a few sentences are demarcated correctly and there is some correct use of commas as well as some comma-splicing of sentences. Handwriting is unclear in places.

Overall comment

This piece is generally clear and tries to include some potentially interesting events in its attempt at an appropriate narrative form, but the inaccuracies and lack of grammatically complex sentences keep it at the lower end of Level 4.

Key Considerations

- some potentially interesting narrative;
- limited sentence construction;
- some accurate sentence punctuation.

Level: 4-   *Mark: 8*

Example 27

This pupil has written on topic b.

I stepped toward the cave door quietly, gun out, ready for anything, I got there nothing was moving not even the tops of the highest trees and it was getting dark so I camped in the cave. I heard the howls of wolf, the cantering of wild horses and the loud snarts of wild-boars. There was the sudden shot of a shot gun and a shout,

"Did you hit it?"

"I'm not sure the furry thing ran into the forest"

"Come on it's cold, lets go"

I was still standing by a tree and it went silent again, I was awake for the rest of the night listening.

It was still dark in the forest and it was about 2.15 am when a loud raw and the sound of a wild-bore being slaughtered, I closed my eyes and listened then opened them and moved toward the sound.

I ran to the camp and the noise died down and stopped, I went further into the cave and made a fire as it was getting cold.

I had fallen asleep and was awoken by something brushing past me it was a man in the doorway I could just see the outline. He looked really hairy and I reached for my gun, the bear looking man ran toward me grabbed one of my legs and picked me off the floor by it.

I was really scared I almost cried but I had to keep calm, then I remembered those men who shot at something furry.

The beast whaled and dropped me, I was still conscious as I backed away toward the door, I had to do something I was scared so much I could not go for my gun I stood frozen in the shadows as he came toward me again and he raued in my ear and I made a dash for it.

I still roam the forest where I last saw the beast but I have not seen him, The sounds have been heard of animals being slaughted, the animals bones are found but not the beast he is a mystery in the forest one minute and out the next.

I still meet other animals that are frightening but not as bad as the beast.

Example 27

Communication of ideas and impact on reader

This piece is clearly expressed and is structured as a narrative, with the first sentence taking the reader straight into the situation, and the final section bringing the reader back to the present as the narrator reflects on his or her experience. The pupil tries to engage the reader's interest through the pace of the narrative and some vigorous use of language, for example, 'cantering of wild horses', 'slaughtered', 'brushing past me', although at other times choice of vocabulary is more predictable.

Structure and accuracy, including grammar, spelling and punctuation.

The story is organised into a clear structure, supported by paragraphs. Simple and complex sentences are used and these are sometimes punctuated correctly although in places there is less control over sentence structure and some comma-splicing. Nevertheless, the dialogue is correctly laid out and punctuated. The spelling is generally secure although there are errors in homophones such as 'raw' and other errors in patterns such as 'cryed' and more demanding words such as 'constious'.

Overall comment

The initial impression of this piece might be of an unconvincing and unoriginal narrative of limited value. However, a more thoughtful consideration reveals an attempt to engage the reader's attention through its structure and pace. There is a reasonable degree of accuracy and control, although the punctuation of sentences is not entirely secure. On a 'best-fit' basis, this response merits an award in the Level 5 band.

Key Considerations

- appropriate narrative structure, supported by paragraphs;
- some accurate use of a range of punctuation, with weaknesses in sentence punctuation;
- reasonably wide vocabulary with generally accurate spelling.

Level: 5   Mark: 16

Example 28

This pupil has written on topic b.

I was on holiday in Northumbria. We were staying in an old farmhouse in the middle of nowhere. We had hired out some mountain bikes and decided to go for a ride. After about a mile of riding ~~through~~ along gravel Tracks in some dark woods we came to a gate. The other side was a wide flat area in between two high cliffs. In the bottom of this 'valley' there was a herd of highland cows. They were huge, they had huge long, sharp horns and long shaggy hair. As we arrived every one of them turned their heads to look at us. The other side of the 'valley' was ~~so~~ more forest and a gate leading to another track. We weren't quite sure what to do next. My uncle was with us and he will Try anything so he decided for us that we would cross the 'valley' one by one. He went first, he just rode, slowly and camly straight through the middle of the cows and they just looked at him! Then my Mum,

Dad and Brother went one by one. My cousin and myself were left. We decided to go together so we opened the gate and started the long ride accross the valley. I could see my uncle looking cross on the other side and when we were right in the middle of the cows he shouted out "come on hurry up, what are you doing?" A bull that we were right next to stood up and snorted, more cows started standing up and they started chasing us. We rode as fast as we could but they seemed to be catching us. We rode faster towards the gate and shouted "open it" we rode even faster and just made it through. The gate slammed shut!

Example 28

Communication of ideas and impact on reader

This is an interesting and engaging narrative with a tense and effective ending. Skilful scene setting involving the use of descriptive detail – 'old farmhouse in the middle of no where'; 'gravel tracks in some dark woods'; 'wide flat area in between two high cliffs'– adds to the vividness of the experience. Incident is described clearly and with some attempt to recreate a sense of excitement and danger with well-chosen details ('every one of them turned their heads to look at us'). The mixture of humour ('he will try anything') and tension ('we weren't quite sure what to do next') works well and helps produce a successful narrative.

Structure and accuracy, including grammar, spelling and punctuation

The narrative is appropriately structured with a setting of the scene followed by a build-up of the sense of danger. A range of sentences is used, including the climactic 'The gate slamned shut!'. Although there is a lack of paragraphs, the piece is clear and the punctuation is usually accurate. There are occasional spelling errors, such as 'camly' and 'accross', but the handwriting is fluent and legible.

Overall comment

The absence of paragraphing may initially suggest a mark in the Level 5 range. However, the engaging nature of the writing, its generally accurate use of spelling and punctuation and its sense of control of structure, despite the lack of paragraphing, justify a mark in the Level 6 range.

Key Considerations

- interesting and engaging in parts;
- appropriate controlled structure;
- accurate apart from paragraphs.

Level: 6   *Mark: 22*

Example 29

This pupil has written on topic b.

The encounter I am going to write about happened about an four years ago in the summer holidays.

It was late in the afternoon, about four o'clock, on a very hot sunny a wednesday. I was just coming back from an excellent afternoon of playing football with my friends. I had just said goodbye to David, Gareth and Jonathan when I began walking up a lane towards my house. I often walked up the lane but this time for some reason it felt different.

On the way up the lane I passed a few people I knew. We stopped and chatted for a while, said goodbye and then carried on our seperate ways. The walk was the same as usual until as I was coming towards the end of it a huge rotweiler type of dog jumped high over the fence and landed about five metres in front of me.

I was terrified! I couldn't just turn around and go the other way because I had kicked my soccer ball ahead of me and was metre or two the other side of the dog.

I didn't know what to do next. Should I go around and come back later? No, I couldn't do that I was going out and the ball may get stolen. Should I make a run for it? No, that was too dangerous.

By this time the dog was growling ferociously and I had decided to just stand absolutely still until the dog moved towards me.

> Suddenly the dog darted this way I was panicking and didn't know what to do. Then the Idea hit me I jumped over the garden of the Jones and hoped for the best. Luckily the dog was running towards its owner who, unoticed, had walked up behind me and asked what was going on. I told him he apologised and I grabbed my ball and ran all the way home.

Example 29

Communication of ideas and impact on reader

This competent and assured narrative engages the reader with its build-up of suspense ('but this time for some reason it felt different') and realistic details ('I passed a few people I knew. We stopped and chatted for a while ...'; 'The walk was the same as usual ...'). Interest and pace are sustained by the narrator sharing his problems ('Should I ...? No, that was too dangerous'). The danger of the situation sounds convincing ('a huge rotweiler') and believable, and the attempt at humour with the bathos of the ending, although not handled entirely successfully, provides an appropriate conclusion.

Structure and accuracy, including grammar, spelling and punctuation

This piece of writing demonstrates control, a range of grammatical features including complex sentences such as the one beginning 'Luckily the dog was running towards its owner ...' and effective use of questions. The vocabulary is appropriate rather than sophisticated. Punctuation and paragraphing clarify the sequence of events, and spelling of difficult words, such as 'ferociously' and 'absolutely', is mostly correct. Handwriting is in a fluent and legible style.

Overall comment

This pupil has produced a realistic and engaging narrative in a confident and controlled style. The overall accuracy adds to the success of the writing and a mark in the Level 7 range is justified.

Key Considerations

- confident and engaging;
- range of grammatical features;
- accurate and controlled.

Level: 7   *Mark: 28*

Example 30

This pupil has written on topic b.

I pulled my coat even tighter around my body, trying to protect me from the cold wind with sliced through my body. I kept my eyes focused on the light, now distant. As long as I kept walking and tried not to think about the fact that I was on my own, and in the dark, I'd be allright.

My car had broken down and I had to get home, it wasn't far, only twenty minutes walk, but in the January cold and darkness, it seemed too long, far too long.

I started humming a tune from a television soap to keep my mind on something other than the situation I was in. Crack! I stopped humming and moving abruptly as I heard a noise, behind me. I stood still, holding my breath, and waiting not knowing which way to turn or where the noise had come from. I waited, but nothing made a sound, all I could hear was cars in the distance, how hard I wished one was here, now. Then it moved, it's eyes, green and bright, glared at me as it sprung from the hedge and scuttled on up the lane, chasing a mouse or small creature of some sort. I let out my breath and sighed, it had only been a cat. My pulse kept on racing as I continued to walk, I was conscious of every small sound, my breath sounded so loud and hands felt so clammy as I shoved them deeper into my coat pocket.

I started going over my tables in my head, like I'd done as a schoolgirl, before a test.

Then twigs crackled and there was a distant thump, thump, thump, thump, on the ground.

My throat went tight, I needed to swallow and breathe.

I forced myself to turn to where the noise was coming from and saw —, nothing but darkness, near pitch black.

Then a shape, an odd looking one, came closer, and grew bigger.

I tried to scream or speak or run, but I could do nothing. I was frozen to the spot.

"Hello?" "Do you need any help, I just saw your car and came to see if you were all right." An attractive man with a dog on a lead came into what moonlight there was.

I let out a sigh and felt like collapsing after the fright that had been through my soul. "Yeah, I'm okay".

"You look a little pale, and cold. Do you want a lift?"

I looked up at him skeptically, what

if he was a weirdo? He sensed my hesitation!

"I know, your Cassandra Barnes, right? I taught you at secondary school for a while. Remember Mr Corbet?"

I smiled, a smile of relief, my old technology teacher, and someone to give me a lift.

"I'd love a lift" I replied as I got into his car and shut the door, also shutting out the wind and my fear too.

Example 30

Communication of ideas and impact on reader

This pupil immediately attempts to generate narrative interest with a tense opening statement: 'I pulled my coat even tighter around my body ...'. A sense of mystery is sustained by 'As long as I kept walking and tried not to think ...' with situations and motives left unstated until the second paragraph. Narrative energy is maintained by the precise description of the writer's actions and responses at each point and the use of two climaxes to the story, the encounter with the cat and then the final meeting with the dog and its owner. The ending neatly encapsulates the resolution of the whole piece in the closing of the car door 'also shutting out the wind and my fear too'.

Structure and accuracy, including grammar, spelling and punctuation

This piece of writing has a clear structure, supported by appropriate use of paragraphing. A variety of sentence structures is employed, using short phrases, and expansion of points to good effect in generating tension (for example: 'My throat went tight, I needed to swallow, and breathe' and 'Then a shape, an odd looking one, came closer, and grew bigger'). A range of punctuation devices is used to support and clarify meaning. Spelling is generally accurate and handwriting is in a fluent and legible style.

Overall comment

This pupil makes a real attempt to create tension and interest through the use of a range of narrative devices, including the effective choice of vocabulary and sentence structures. Paragraphing and punctuation are also helpfully employed in support of an engaging piece of writing. There are one or two errors, but these are not typical of the piece and overall this is a coherent and distinctive narrative that just fulfils the requirements for a mark in the range above Level 7.

Key Considerations

- coherent narrative making distinctive and effective use of a range of stylistic effects;
- high level of technical accuracy.

Level: above 7-   *Mark: 31*

Fold out this flap for the performance criteria for Question 4b.

Q. No 4b Marks available 33	Write about a frightening encounter with an animal. You could: • write about a real or imaginary event; • try to build up a feeling of tension or suspense.		
Performance Criteria		**Level**	**Mark**
Some of the pupils' ideas are clearly expressed and their writing has some features which are appropriate to a story or piece of personal writing. The piece has shape and an ending. The basic grammatical structure of some sentences is correct and some punctuation is used accurately. The spelling of simple words is usually accurate and the handwriting is mostly legible, though there may be obvious weaknesses in the formation of some letters.		- below 4 +	2 4 6
The pupils' ideas are generally clear and mostly organised in a narrative or other appropriate form. There is some use of grammatically complex sentences and pupils are beginning to use descriptive words effectively. Punctuation to mark sentences is mostly used accurately and pupils are beginning to use punctuation within the sentence. The spelling of simple and common polysyllabic words is generally accurate. Handwriting is mostly clear and legible.		- 4 +	8 10 12
The pupils' writing is clearly expressed and structured in a narrative or other appropriate form. Pupils try to engage the reader's interest by such means as expression of feelings, or description of character, animal or setting. A reasonably wide vocabulary is used though some words may not be used precisely. Simple and complex sentences are usually organised into a clear structure or paragraphs. A range of punctuation, including commas, apostrophes and speech marks, is usually used accurately. Spelling, including that of words with complex regular patterns, is usually accurate. Handwriting is generally clear and legible in a fluent style.		- 5 +	14 16 18
The pupils' writing is interesting and engaging in parts, using an appropriate style and form to present feelings, events, characters or setting. A varied vocabulary, a range of simple and complex sentences and appropriate paragraphing contribute to the effectiveness of the writing, though the same quality may not be evident throughout. A range of punctuation is usually used correctly to clarify meaning. Spelling is accurate though there may be some errors in difficult words. Handwriting is in a fluent and legible style.		- 6 +	20 22 24
The pupils' writing is confident, organised and written in an appropriate and engaging style. Although the subject matter may be relatively unsophisticated, narrative interest is built up by a range of grammatical features and the effective use of vocabulary. Paragraphing and correct punctuation are used to make the sequence of events in the narrative clear. Spelling, including that of complex irregular words, is correct. Handwriting is in a fluent and legible style.		- 7 +	26 28 30
The pupils' writing engages and maintains the interest of the reader by presenting a coherent narrative with distinctive structural or stylistic effects. The precise use of a range of vocabulary and grammatical structures enables clarity and emphasis to be achieved. Pupils show a consistent grasp of the correct use of paragraphing and a range of punctuation. Spelling, including that of complex irregular words, is correct. Handwriting is in a fluent and legible style.		- above 7 +	31 32 33

QUESTION 4b

Assessment Objectives

This question assesses pupils' ability to:

- communicate ideas to a reader;

- use an appropriate style;

- organise their writing appropriately for their chosen form;

- shape and develop their work using paragraphs, grammatical structures and punctuation to convey their meaning;

- choose words precisely and imaginatively and to spell them correctly;

- write clearly and legibly.

> **This task allows pupils the freedom to write in whatever form they believe to be appropriate. Be prepared to reward succinct or unusual but effective responses.**
>
> **Keep looking for evidence of positive achievement and if you think a response clearly deserves a particular level, place it securely in that level.**

Reminder

Use the performance criteria opposite in conjunction with the exemplar responses to assess the qualities of an answer on a 'best-fit' basis. You should make a judgement of the overall qualities of the answer. Weaknesses in one area can be compensated for by strengths in another.

Please refer to page 8 of this mark scheme for guidance on marking the work of pupils who have used an amanuensis or a mechanical aid such as a word processor.

Example 31

The trees in the rain forest
are mostley tall and ~~the~~ high
quality ltwood ~~so~~ people are
chooping them down. This was
ok but. every year the are
vast areas of trees disapearing
not only are we going to run
out of would but they take carbon
dioxide out of the air.

But do not forget the or still
people that live in the rain
forests its like running them
out of ltherse homes
plus there are still animals
plus more animals and plant
that do not grow any were
else

Example 31

Communication of ideas and impact on reader

This is a brief response which has no recognisable features of a speech in the opening paragraph. The second paragraph, however, does address the reader directly and there is an attempt in the piece to present views although these are undeveloped and the response both begins and ends rather abruptly.

Structure and accuracy, including grammar, spelling and punctuation

The first sentence is grammatically correct and accurately punctuated. Thereafter, however, although the pupil tries to use complex sentences, they are not always controlled or demarcated by capital letters and full stops. Simple words, such as 'forest' and 'every' are spelled correctly but there are errors in words such as 'chooping' and 'any were'; 'disapearing', a more demanding word, is also misspelt. The handwriting is clear and legible, though not joined.

Overall comment

This is a brief response which does not show enough evidence of appropriate form or tone to fulfil the Level 4 criteria. However, there is some attempt at an appropriate form and there are some accurate sentences which justify a mark in the range below Level 4.

Key Considerations

* brief, limited response;
* some accurate sentence structures with appropriate punctuation;
* little evidence of appropriate form and tone of a speech.

Level: below 4-   Mark: 2

Example 32

This pupil has written on topic c.

Hunting is a big issue alot of people dont like. people ride around on horses shooting animals for no major reason. They take there hunting dog's with them. In this world there is two much cruelty to animals and then people go around hunting. You need to think carefully about hunting. why do they do it? What do they get~~m~~ out of killing animals for no apparent reason? If you know anyone who does hunting ask them questions they probably wont have straight answers. Because they find it fun to kill animals. Hunting should not be allowed and people should understand this and not ignore the issue as I speak people are going around hunting and killing all those animals.

Example 32

Communication of ideas and impact on reader

This pupil's response begins appropriately with 'Hunting is a big issue' and tries to maintain this tone with rhetorical questions and a suitable ending ('people should ... not ignore the issue'). It may be claimed that statements such as 'people ride around on horses shooting animals ...' may be exaggerated for effect, but this actually reflects the limited development of the opinions presented. This is a short speech and it becomes very generalised, but it is, on the whole, clear and readable.

Structure and accuracy, including grammar, spelling and punctuation

This piece is reasonably well organised into a sequence of statements and questions to put across the pupil's opinions. Punctuation to mark sentences is generally accurate. Some polysyllabic words are spelled accurately ('carefully', 'understand') while there are errors in homophones ('there', 'two'). Handwriting is clear and legible.

Overall comment

Although this is a short response, there is just sufficient evidence of an appropriate tone and clarity of expression to merit a mark in the Level 4 range.

Key Considerations

- attempts appropriate form;
- generally clear;
- generalised rather than developed opinions.

Level: 4-   *Mark: 8*

Example 33

This pupil has written on topic c.

I feel strongly about Animal Experimentation.
I think that it is wrong to test cosmetics
and house-hold goods [medicines] on animals. I don't
think a lot of people know what really
goes on. Not all companies and shops
test their products on animals such as
The Body Shop which also feels strongly
about this topic.

People shave rodents hair off and
would smear cream over it's skin.
If this red rodent's skin came up all
red or sore then they would know
they would have to investigate this
cream into more detail further. Sometimes
this experimenting can lead to death for
these poor animals.

How would you like it if someone
came along and injected a drug into
you which could be very lefal! You
could end up dead. How would you feel
if you didn't have any choice?

A human ear was grown on a rat
before. Imagine having to carry an ear
on your back. Would you like it? I don't
think I would. I know that you wouldn't

want to buy anything dangerous which could have an affect on you but why test them on other animals. They have the same rights as we do. The animals aren't kept in good conditions either.

Animals often don't get enough food or water which they need to have. Often there are several rodents kept in one cage which isn't very hygenic. So please, think next time you buy a product that could of been tested on animals check that it hasn't before buying it, because that's how you can help!

Example 33

Communication of ideas and impact on reader

This is a straightforward response with a direct expression of a point of view. It makes a direct appeal to the reader using some forms of expression appropriate to a speech ('How would you like it if ...'; 'Imagine having to ...'). The overall effect is of a number of relevant points on the subject rather than a tightly argued and coherently structured piece of polemic, but some attempt is made to achieve an appropriate form and tone.

Structure and accuracy, including grammar, spelling and punctuation

This piece of writing is clearly expressed with points organised into paragraphs. Vocabulary is used precisely to convey meaning and there is some variety of sentence structures. Repetition of devices such as 'How would you ...' and emphasis on the writer's own views – 'I think ...' – are quite acceptable in the context of the task. There are occasional technical errors – 'of' for 'have'; a misplaced apostrophe in 'its' – but otherwise spelling and punctuation are nearly always accurate.

Overall comment

This is a straightforward, clearly expressed response to the task, with very few errors. All aspects of Level 5 performance are evident and so a mark in that band is justified.

Key Considerations

- direct and clear expression of a point of view;
- straightforward statement of ideas;
- few technical errors.

Level: 5+   *Mark: 18*

Example 34

This pupil has written on topic c.

I am here to talk about blood sports. I, like many others believe that blood sports are cruel and totally uneseccary. It seems totally sick that anybody can get fun out of killing a defencless animal, even if it is not killed the chase will have had phsycological effects on the animal, as it has recently been proven.

Lets look at it this way. You are out in a field doing nothing much, perhaps to picking berries to make a jam with. Suddenly from through the gate a pack of hounds runs, you can see they are after you and you start to run, to start with you have an advantage on them, you are a good sprinter and can out pace them easily, but they are still chasing you. You can sprint but you haven't got the stamina for long distance and you starts to slow, because you just can't keep up the pace. The hounds begin to gain on you and you try to push harder but you can't manage it. The hounds are right on your tail now but you keep on running. There is a log in front of you and the only way to go is over it, your tired but you try to jump, not quite high enough. You tumble to the ground, the dogs are on you, are panting, you feel numb but you still feel the imence pain as the dogs bite into you.

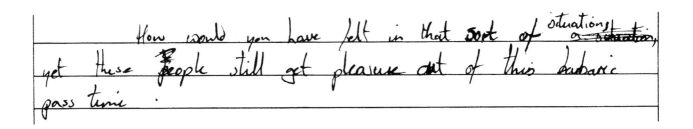

How would you have felt in that sort of situation, yet these People still get pleasure out of this barbaric pass time .

Example 34

Communication of ideas and impact on reader

This pupil shows good awareness of audience, attempting to engage interest by describing a reversed-role situation in detail. The appropriate tone ('I, like many others ...', 'Lets look at it this way') controlled organisation and build-up of a sense of drama add to the effectiveness of the piece. However, the ending is rather abrupt, leaving the reader with a sense that the piece could have been rather more developed.

Structure and accuracy, including grammar, spelling and punctuation

This piece uses effective paragraphing, a range of simple and complex sentences, and a varied vocabulary ('phsycological', 'sprinter', 'tumble', 'panting', 'numb'). Spelling is less successful, with errors such as 'imence', 'beries and 'unesercary', although other complex words are accurately spelled ('advantage', 'pleasure'). Commas are overused in places but the punctuation still clarifies meaning.

Overall comment

The organisation, effective vocabulary and appropriate tone of this piece compensate for the errors in spelling and punctuation. A mark in the Level 6 band is justified.

Key Considerations

- an engaging speech with an appropriate tone;
- some variety of vocabulary and sentence structures, but with technical weaknesses.

Level: 6   *Mark: 22*

Example 35

This pupil has written on topic c.

4. Hello. The subject that I want to talk about this morning is the use of nuclear weapons in a war. I feel very strongly about this subject because I have seen many pictures of the horrific devastation caused by these doomsday weapons, possessing enough power to destroy a city and to completely flatten each and every one of its buildings. But even though this would be bad enough, nuclear weapons' most horrible effects are on people. People near the explosion of the warhead are turned into nothing more than a pile of ash, but also the people who are not killed sustain horrible injuries. 'Radiation burns' as these injuries are called, can last someone for their whole life and cause great pain. These injuries rarely seal up and cannot usually be treated. They sometimes prove lethal to people. Also, people furthest away from the blast may get radiation into their bodies and die as it destroys their bodies from the insides. This death is slow and painful, lasting weeks or months. People with radiation sickness often cough up blood and often suffer painful spasms. To prevent this happening to anyone else, the people of the world should tell their governments that they are firmly opposed to nuclear weapons and make demonstrations. Some governments in the world have no nuclear warheads, but most do. If just one missile was launched, the entire world could be made into a nuclear wasteland as every country fired missiles at other countries, destroying most of the world's capital cities and killing billions and billions of people. Although this is not likely to happen, if just one dictator fired a nuclear weapon the world would be shaken, millions or even billions could die, and this could spark off a nuclear war which is the worst thing that could happen to the world. This affects you because nuclear war, even if everyone didn't die, would reduce civilisation back to the Middle Ages in terms of technology and you would have no chance of going to university, getting a well paid job or doing something important with your life. So,

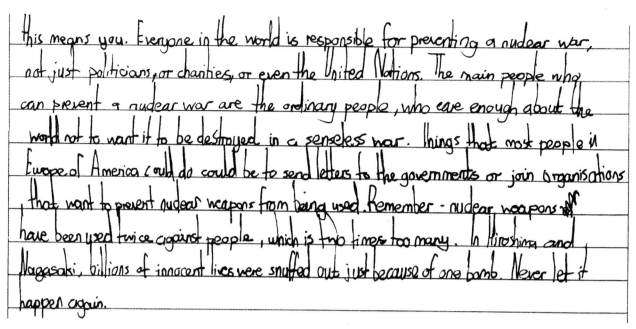

this means you. Everyone in the world is responsible for preventing a nuclear war, not just politicians, or charities, or even the United Nations. The main people who can prevent a nuclear war are the ordinary people, who care enough about the world not to want it to be destroyed in a senseless war. Things that most people in Europe or America could do could be to send letters to the governments or join organisations that want to prevent nuclear weapons from being used. Remember - nuclear weapons have been used twice against people, which is two times too many. In Hiroshima and Nagasaki, billions of innocent lives were snuffed out just because of one bomb. Never let it happen again.

Example 35

Communication of ideas and impact on reader

This controlled and well-informed piece tends to read as a well-argued piece of writing rather than a speech. However, the pupil does begin and end ('Never let it happen again') with a sense of audience and there are also reminders such as 'So, this means you' and 'Everyone in the world is responsible' to engage the reader. The writing is confident, well organised and convincing.

Structure and accuracy, including grammar, spelling and punctuation

This piece has no paragraph demarcation, but there is a sense of overall control and organisation and this pupil confidently uses a range of grammatical features. Vocabulary is very varied and appropriately powerful to influence the reader ('painful spasms', 'reduce civilisation', 'destroyed in a senseless war'). Complex sentences and accurate punctuation and spelling add to the success of the piece. Handwriting is dense but legible.

Overall comment

This piece presents the argument well, and it is carefully organised and accurate. Its confident and appropriate tone make an impact on the reader, and it merits a mark in the Level 7 range.

Key Considerations

- confident, appropriate tone;
- effective vocabulary;
- range of grammatical features.

Level: 7   *Mark: 28*

Example 36

This pupil has written on topic c.

4.C I have decided to take this opportunity to tell you about a subject I feel strongly about. Recently, there has been discussion as to whether to ban hunting in Britain. Several views have been put forward, and I would like to tell you what I think on the subject.

Fox and deer hunting has been tradionally part of English life since medevial times, and many organizations still practise it, often with several reasons for doing so. For instance, many pro-hunting associations claim that animals like foxes are vermin, pests. They steal from farms and cause havoc with chickens, hens and so on. Apparently, hunting only helps to keep numbers down. However, I think that this is only an excuse to hide the real reason for hunting - Sport. People are killing defenceless animals for no other reason than that they enjoy the "thrill of the hunt". I find it impossible to believe that anyone could enjoy watching a helpless fox be ripped limb from limb by starved hounds. Surely, if foxes must be killed, then there must be more humane ways of doing it. Also, from the practical side of things, it would be far cheaper to send out a team of men with tranquilliser darts, and they would accomplish more in an hour, than an expensive organized hunt could do in a week.

Also, someone suggested that animals like deer enjoy the thrill of the chase through woodlands and forests, and personally, I think this is the most preposterous claim I have ever heard.

How can any animal enjoy running for it's life desperately, while baying hounds and men with guns give chase? Often, the animal collapses before it is caught, upon which it is set upon by the dogs. I'm sorry if this seems a little dramatic, but I think it is important to tell you exactly what goes on in these barbaric events.

If enough people think as I do, then we can stop hunting for good. The government is considering the ban, and if enough public support is gained, we can put an end to the slaughter of innocent animals, for good. Every second that we stand by and ignore what is happening, another animals' life is wasted, it is needless, barbaric and tragic that animals are killed for no purpose, but you have the power to stop it.

Example 36

Communication of ideas and impact on reader

From the opening paragraph, where the pupil introduces the topic and makes it clear that it is a speech, this piece engages and maintains the interest of the reader. The arguments put forward are not particularly original, but they are well expressed, linked and structured so that the reader is borne along by them. There is a balance between evidence and personal opinion with reference to the audience throughout the speech and some use of rhetorical features: 'Surely, if foxes must be killed, then there must be more humane ways of doing it.' It ends with a rallying cry to the audience to use their influence to stop hunting: 'it is needless, barbaric and tragic that animals are killed for no purpose, but <u>you</u> have the power to stop it.'

Structure and accuracy, including grammar, spelling and punctuation

This speech is coherently structured with appropriate use of paragraphs to support that structure. The sentence structures are varied, well controlled and often used to clarify and emphasise meaning: for example, 'However, I think that this is only an excuse to hide the real reason for hunting – sport' and 'The government is considering the ban, and if enough public support is gained, we can put an end to the slaughter of innocent animals, for good.' A range of punctuation, including commas, dashes and inverted commas, is used correctly and the pupil also uses a range of polysyllabic words, including 'tradionally', 'accomplish', 'preposterous' and 'barbaric', which is mostly spelled correctly.

Overall comment

This is a coherent and well-expressed piece which effectively conveys a point of view in the form of a speech. It is not entirely accurate – for example, 'apparantly', as the pupil has spelt it, is misspelt and the apostrophe in 'animals'' is misplaced. Nevertheless, the strengths of the piece in terms of its structure, control and use of grammatical features and vocabulary mean that it gains the award of a mark in the range above Level 7.

Key Considerations

- engages and maintains the interest of the reader;
- coherently structured with an effective use of grammatical features and vocabulary;
- mostly accurate use of punctuation and spelling.

Level: above 7   *Mark: 32*

Fold out this flap for the performance criteria for Question 4c.

Q. No 4c	The leaflet you have read tries to change people's opinions about wolves.		
Marks available 33	Imagine you have been given a chance to talk in a year assembly. Choose an issue you feel strongly about. (It does not need to be about animals.) **Write your speech trying to persuade other people to support your views.**		

Performance Criteria	Level	Mark
Some of the pupils' ideas are clearly expressed, and their writing shows some features which are appropriate to a speech. The basic grammatical structure of some sentences is correct and some punctuation is used accurately. The spelling of simple words is usually accurate and the handwriting is mostly legible, though there may be obvious weaknesses in the formation of some letters.	- below 4 +	2 4 6
The pupils' ideas are generally clear and mostly organised in an appropriate form for a speech. Sentence structures and vocabulary are beginning to be used to create an appropriate tone for a speech, although this may not be maintained. Punctuation to mark sentences is mostly used accurately and pupils are beginning to use punctuation within the sentence. The spelling of simple and common polysyllabic words is generally accurate. Handwriting is mostly clear and legible.	- 4 +	8 10 12
The pupils' writing is clearly expressed and the points are organised in an appropriate form for a speech, usually with a clear structure or paragraphs. Pupils try to engage and persuade the audience by such means as giving examples to illustrate their points. The choice of vocabulary and sentence structures contributes to an appropriate tone for a speech, although this may not be maintained. A range of punctuation, including commas and apostrophes, is usually used accurately. Spelling, including that of words with complex regular patterns, is usually accurate. Handwriting is generally clear and legible in a fluent style.	- 5 +	14 16 18
Pupils use an appropriate style and tone for a speech presenting a point of view and their writing is interesting and engaging in parts. A varied vocabulary, a range of simple and complex sentences and appropriate paragraphing contribute to the effectiveness of the writing, although the same quality may not be evident throughout. A range of punctuation is usually used correctly to clarify meaning. Spelling is accurate though there may be some errors in difficult words. Handwriting is in a fluent and legible style.	- 6 +	20 22 24
The pupils' writing is confident, organised and written in an appropriate tone, style and form to argue a case. Although the pupils' views may be relatively unsophisticated, the audience is presented with some of the arguments clearly by a range of grammatical features and the effective use of vocabulary. Paragraphing and correct punctuation are used to make the sequence of ideas clear. Spelling, including that of complex irregular words, is correct. Handwriting is in a fluent and legible style.	- 7 +	26 28 30
The pupils' writing engages and maintains the interest of the audience by presenting arguments clearly in a coherent way. The precise use of a range of vocabulary and grammatical structures enables clarity and emphasis to be achieved. Pupils show a consistent grasp of the correct use of paragraphing and a range of punctuation. Spelling, including that of complex irregular words, is correct. Handwriting is in a fluent and legible style.	- above 7 +	31 32 33

QUESTION 4c

Assessment Objectives

This question assesses pupils' ability to:

- communicate ideas to a reader;

- use an appropriate style;

- organise their writing appropriately for their chosen form;

- shape and develop their work using paragraphs, grammatical structures and punctuation to convey their meaning;

- choose words precisely and imaginatively and to spell them correctly;

- write neatly and legibly.

> **It is important to be flexible in interpreting what constitutes an appropriate style and form for this option. Pupils should be rewarded for their ability to include interesting and convincing ideas, put together an argument effectively and sustain their chosen style and form. In some cases pupils may write briefly; look for quality not quantity and reward the effective, if succinct, response.**
>
> **At the lower levels a direct expression of a point of view, with, for instance, some use of examples to develop the argument or some involvement of the audience would be appropriate. Pupils' writing at the higher levels will use a range of stylistic features appropriate to a speech, such as rhetorical devices.**
>
> **Keep looking for evidence of positive achievement and if you think a response clearly deserves a particular level, place it securely in that level.**

Reminder

Use the performance criteria opposite in conjunction with the exemplar responses to assess the qualities of an answer on a 'best-fit' basis. You should make a judgement of the overall qualities of the answer. Weaknesses in one area can be compensated for by strengths in another.

Please refer to page 8 of this mark scheme for guidance on marking the work of pupils who have used an amanuensis or a mechanical aid such as a word processor.

Additional guidance for Paper 2

On the following pages each of the six alternative tasks in Paper 2 has its own performance criteria, examplar answers and indicative content.

Each task must be marked twice, once for Understanding and Response and then again for Written Expression.

Please note that each task has a set of Written Expression criteria next to the criteria for Understanding and Response. There are different criteria for Tasks 2 and 4, which require pupils to write empathetically. Some minor adjustments have also been made to the criteria for Task 3 to clarify what is appropriate for writing in response to this directing task.

Keep looking for evidence of positive achievement. If you think an answer deserves a particular level, place it securely into that level.

Assessment objectives

The tasks in Paper 2 assess pupil's ability to understand and respond to:

- Shakespeare's presentation of ideas;

- the motivation and behaviour of characters;

- the development of plot;

- the language of the scenes;

- the overall impact of the scenes;

- the presentation of the scenes on stage.

Also assessed in this paper will be pupils' ability to:

- write in a style appropriate to the task;

- organise writing clearly, using paragraphs where appropriate;

- use grammatical structures and vocabulary suitable for the clear and precise expression of meaning;

- use a variety of sentence structures;

- use accurate punctuation and spelling;

- write clearly and legibly.

Example	Task	Level exemplified		Page number
		U/R	W/E	
1	Julius Caesar Task 1	below 4	4-	96
2	Julius Caesar Task 1	5	5-	98
3	Julius Caesar Task 1	7	6+	102
Performance Criteria for Julius Caesar Task 1				108
4	Julius Caesar Task 2	4+	4-	110
5	Julius Caesar Task 2	6-	6-	113
6	Julius Caesar Task 2	7	7	116
Performance Criteria for Julius Caesar Task 2				120
7	A Midsummer Night's Dream Task 3	4	5	122
8	A Midsummer Night's Dream Task 3	5	5-	126
9	A Midsummer Night's Dream Task 3	6	6	130
10	A Midsummer Night's Dream Task 3	7+	7	135
Performance Criteria for A Midsummer Night's Dream Task 3				142
11	A Midsummer Night's Dream Task 4	below 4	below 4	144
12	A Midsummer Night's Dream Task 4	5+	5	145
13	A Midsummer Night's Dream Task 4	6	5	148
14	A Midsummer Night's Dream Task 4	7	6+	153
Performance Criteria for A Midsummer Night's Dream Task 4				156
15	Romeo and Juliet Task 5	4+	4	158
16	Romeo and Juliet Task 5	6	6	162
17	Romeo and Juliet Task 5	7-	7	167
Performance Criteria for Romeo and Juliet Task 5				172
18	Romeo and Juliet Task 6	4	4+	174
19	Romeo and Juliet Task 6	5	5-	177
20	Romeo and Juliet Task 6	6-	5+	180
21	Romeo and Juliet Task 6	above 7	above 7	185
Performance Criteria for Romeo and Juliet Task 6				190

Example 1

Julius Caesar, Act 1 Scene 2, Task 1.

~~The Scene Starts with Caesar~~ the different ways in which Cassius tries to persuade Brutus to join the plott are as follows: Cassius choices this moment to speak to Brutus because the Games are on Cassius starts the to speak to Brutus by saying "Will you go see the order of the Cause." Brutus replies ~~n~~ "I am not gamesome". Cassius starts to persuade Brutus by saying "you bear to stubborn and too strange." Cassius is trying to worm his way into Brutus and get him to join the plot Cassius has much to say to get Brutus. ~~Cassius thinks that he should be asking more than Caesar because he had to he Starts to explain to Brutus~~ Then Brutus and Cassius here flourish and Shouting coming from the square Brutus Quotes by saying "WHAT MEANS THIS SHOUTING? I DO FEAR THE PEOPLE CHOOSE CAESAR FOR THEIR KING." Cassius talking about Caesar and that he Sould'nt Be King because as Cassius Quotes "THE TROUBLED TIBER CHAFING WITH HER SHORES Caesar Said to me, 'Dar'st thou, Cassius NOW LEAP IN WITH ME INTO THIS ANGRY FLOOD AND SWIM TO YOUNDER POINT?' Upon THE WORD, ACCOURTED AS I WAS, I PLUNGED IN AND BADE N FOLLOW; SO INDEED HE DID. THE TORRENT ROARED, AND WE DID BUFFET IT WITH LUSTY SINEWS, THROWING IT ASIDE AND STEMMING IT WITH HEARTS OF CONTROUSEY. BUT ERE WE COULD ARRIVE THE POINT PROPOSED CAESAR CRIED, 'HELP ME, CASSIUS, OR I SINK!"/ Cassius then had to Save Caesar and take HIM TO the Shore. Then Cassius goes on to explain that Caesar had a fever in Spain and that he Shake "Tis TRUE, THIS GOD DID SHAKE." his lips turned Colour he then asked FOR DRINK Brutes Could here more SHOUTING and flourish

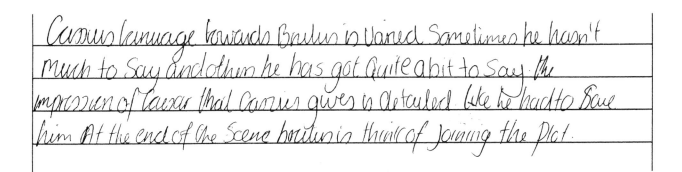

Cassius lanuage towards Brutus is varied. Sometimes he hasn't
much to Say and othem he has got Quite a bit to Say. the
impression of Caesar that Cassius gives is detailed. Like he had to Save
him. At the end of the Scene brutus is think of Joining the Plot.

Example 1

UNDERSTANDING AND RESPONSE

The pupil tends to retell the story of parts of the scene rather unselectively; there is some response to the first prompt ('Cassius choices this moment to speak to Brutus because the Games are on') but no consideration of the way Cassius uses his understanding of Brutus's character. The comment that Cassius 'is trying to worm his way into Brutus' implies some awareness of Cassius's intentions. However, the overlong quotation to illustrate what Cassius thinks of Caesar is given without explanation, and concluded with the vague generalisation about Cassius's speeches: 'Sometimes he hasn't much to say and others he has got Quite a bit to say'. The limited nature of this response means that a mark in the range below Level 4 is appropriate.

Key Considerations

* retells what happens in parts of the scene;
* references given without explanation.

Level: below 4   *Mark: 3*

WRITTEN EXPRESSION

The response is generally clearly expressed using a narrative approach ('Then Cassius gos on to ... '). Sentences are not consistently punctuated and there is no paragraphing. Vocabulary is adequate for this pupil's range of ideas and occasionally suggests the development of a point of view, but spelling is unreliable. Handwriting is mainly clear and legible, despite some inconsistency in the use of upper and lower case. A mark at the bottom of the Level 4 range is justified.

Key Considerations

* limited development and organisation of ideas;
* inconsistent spelling and punctuation.

Level: 4-   *Mark: 4*

Example 2

Julius Caesar, Act 1 Scene 2, Task 1.

I feel that Cassius chose this moment this moment to speak to Brutus because he might have felt a bit weird due to the soothsayer saying 'Beware the Ides of March' to Caesar. Cassius knew Brutus was a good friend of Caesars and thought that if he could get him on his and the other conspirators side they would be an even stronger force. (The didn't really see themselves as murderers, but as protectors of Rome.)

Cassius gives Brutus quite a few reasons why Caesar should not become the emperor of this great city Rome.

Reason One: Himself (Cassius) had gone walking with Caesar on a Winter's cold and gusty day, when they reached the shores of the River Tiber which was roaring and raging and churning the waters.

Caesar jumped in and said "Dar'st thou, Cassius, now leap in with me into this angry flood and swim to yonder point?"
    Cassius did so, but when they had swam half-way across Caesar cried "Help me Cassius, or I will sink."
With these words Cassius put Caesar on his shoulder and swam to shore.

    Then he explains a whole lot of reasons why they shouldn't make him emperor and that they should stop treating him like a god. Then he explained again

Reason 2: Himself (Cassius) and Caesar were alone   (we don't know where) when Caesar (God) started to shake, and started foaming around the lips whilst he grew weaker he started to groan.
    Then said the Great Caesar

        "Alas", it cried "give
        me some drink,
        Titinius"

It sounded like a little girl crying. Then Cassius said

> "Ye gods, it doth amaze
> me a man of such feeble
> temper should so get the
> start of the majestic world
> And bear the palm alone"

So in these two reasons Cassius is trying to give the impression that Caesar is just like any other, commoner in the city

In the first moments of there conversation Cassius speaks to Brutus in a way so that Caesars name is not mentioned and that they want to get rid of him (Caesar). If he had opened with the sentence

> "We want to kill Caesar"

Brutus would have most likely ran off and told the police and Caesar to have Cassius arrested or something. The thing is Cassius chose his words very carefully as so not to give the game away.

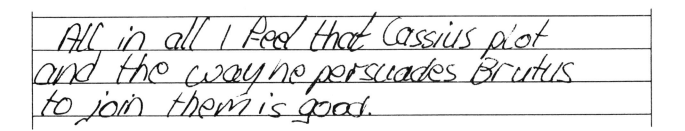

All in all I feel that Cassius plot and the way he persuades Brutus to join them is good.

Example 2

UNDERSTANDING AND RESPONSE

This answer gives an overview of the scene, touching on most aspects of the task. The pupil shows understanding of Cassius's motives for wishing to draw Brutus to his cause and focuses mainly on Caesar's physical inadequacy. There is a large element of narrative and perhaps overuse of quotation to illustrate points. Towards the end of the answer the pupil shows some appreciation of the obliqueness of Cassius's approach, but this is not analysed in any detail. The pupil's ideas and use of quotation are relevant but not developed and so a mark in the Level 5 range is appropriate.

Key Considerations

- overview of the scene;
- understanding of some of the characters' motivation;
- no comment on language.

Level: 5   Mark: 11

WRITTEN EXPRESSION

The response is clearly expressed and some attempt is made to organise and structure ideas by the use of paragraphing and subheadings. Vocabulary is not always used precisely ('he might have felt a bit weird'), but punctuation is reasonably accurate, though apostrophes are not used consistently. There are some errors in common words ('there' for 'their') though more complex words are usually spelled accurately. Handwriting is clear and legible. Overall, therefore, this writing has features of Level 5 performance.

Key Considerations

- ideas generally clearly expressed;
- some attempt at organisation;
- some weaknesses in expression.

Level: 5-   Mark: 7

Example 3

Julius Caesar, Act 1 Scene 2, Task 1.

Cassius is very intelligent and cunning. He knows what he wants and tries hard to get it. In this scene he tries hard to convince Brutus that Caesar is bad and that he will do no good for Rome.

He decides to persuade Brutus while the annual race is going on. He picks that moment because he and Brutus are alone and will not be disturbed as the whole city (mainly) have gone to watch the races. Caesar is also at the races with his guards etc. so they will not be caught.

To start off their conversation Cassius decides to find out what is wrong with Brutus and why he has been so "off" with Cassius.

Cassius asks him in a kind and caring way "Brutus, I do observe you now of late: I have not from your eyes that gentleness and show of love as I was wont to have" Saying this helps to make Brutus open up a bit more to Cassius which would make him more vunerable for Cassius to strike with what he wants to say.

Brutus explains to Cassius that he does not quite know what it is that is troubling him. Cassius spots his chance and very kindly offers to help Brutus to understand his views, and the confusion in his head.

Brutus is a true and loyal republican. He is for the respublica and always will be. Cassius understands this and sort of makes this point Brutus' weak spot, because he knows that if he mentions anything about the respublica, then, Brutus will pay attention and want to listen to what Cassius has to say.

"I have heard where many of the best respect in Rome (Except immortal Caesar), speaking of Brutus and groaning underneath this age's yoke, have wished that noble Brutus had his eyes." Cassius said this to Brutus to help to boost Brutus' confidence up and to explain to him that even though the people of Rome love Caesar greatly they would rather he had Brutus' eyes so that he could see and think of the world and Rome through Brutus' eyes and do things as Brutus does.

The impression that Cassius gives Brutus of Caesar is that Caesar wants too much power and if he was to rule on his own the people of Rome would become Caesars slaves.

Cassius is trying to tell Brutus that he thinks

that Caesar is too weak and feeble to be the ruler of Rome and that Brutus is as good as 'Caesar, if not better. e.g. "I was born as free a Caesar, so were you; we both have fed as well, and we can both endure the winter's cold as well as he."

He explains that Caesar is weak by bringing up some situations in which Caesar was weak and could not handle it.

"Caesar said to me, 'Dar'st thou, Cassius, now leap in with me into this angry flood and swim to yonder point?' Upon the word ....I plunged in and bade him follow; so indeed he did .... Caesar cried, 'Help me, Cassius or I sink!'...... so from the waves of Tiber did I the tired Caesar. And this man is now become a god........"

Another situation in which Caesar was involved Cassius describes Caesar to Brutus "as a sick girl."

Cassius is a very clever man and uses words in a way that intises Brutus into what he has to say about Caesar.

Another way Cassius tells Brutus that he is as good as Caesar is by putting their, sort of, satistics together.

" Brutus and Caesar: What should be in that

'Caesar'? Why should that name be sounded more than yours? Write them together, yours is as fair a name; sound them, it doth become the mouth as well; weigh them, it is as heavy......" etc.

As soon as Cassius mentions Rome he has got Brutus hooked. He talks about it near the end of his speech so that it hits Brutus harder and so that it is the last thing that Brutus hears so it is the last thing he forgets.

"When could they say, till now, that talked of Rome, that her wide walks encompassed but one man?....."

Also in this speech Cassius brings up Brutus' family and the fact that they had always fought for Rome to be a republic which makes Brutus feel that he has to carry on this tradition.

Cassius was very clever and
knew how he could
make Brutus listen
and it worked.

Example 3

UNDERSTANDING AND RESPONSE

This is a detailed and wide-ranging response showing engagement with the text. It focuses well on the ways in which Cassius manipulates Brutus; the pupil's references to the 'respublica' are apt. The pupil shows a clear understanding of the ways in which Cassius presents Caesar's weak points to Brutus. Quotations are well selected and integrated into the essay. Although Cassius's use of language is not commented on explicitly, the selection of key phrases at telling moments, for example, describing Caesar 'as a sick girl' justifies the claim that Cassius is 'a very clever man who uses words in a way that intises Brutus'. A first reading suggests there are some features of an above Level 7 response, but closer analysis shows this is an answer with good understanding rather than one with the insight required at above Level 7.

Key Considerations

- confident and full response;
- good understanding of character and situation;
- well-selected references illustrating use of language.

Level: 7   *Mark: 19*

WRITTEN EXPRESSION

The pupil writes in a generally clear, structured and appropriate style, with a sophisticated vocabulary (vulnerable, entices, res publica) although the spelling of such words is not always secure. An appropriate range of vocabulary is usually employed effectively, although occasionally the pupil has recourse to colloquialisms; 'As soon as Cassius mentions Rome he has got Brutus hooked' may be appropriate in context, but 'some situations in which Caesar was weak and could not handle it' is too colloquial to make meaning precisely clear. The use of paragraphs is effective in shaping the development of the argument. Handwriting is clear and legible throughout a long essay. This piece can therefore be awarded a mark at the top of the Level 6 range.

Key Considerations

- generally clear and appropriate style and organisation;
- varied, interesting vocabulary;
- some spelling errors in complex words.

Level: 6+   *Mark: 12*

> **If pupils follow the events in the scene chronologically, markers will need to recognise 'comment' which may be part of the retelling. Pupils who juxtapose relevant ideas from the scene should be given credit for doing more than merely retelling.**
>
> **Keep looking for evidence of positive achievement and if you think an answer clearly deserves a particular level, place it securely into that level.**

Content

Pupils may refer to some of the following points in their answers. These points do not imply that there is a required content. Pupils may include and develop some of these points, but not necessarily all of them or in this order.

- Cassius seizes on Brutus's words that suggest that Brutus is unhappy about Caesar's style of leadership, such as his behaving like a god.

- Cassius uses his knowledge of Brutus's honesty, integrity and love of his country to persuade him that it is his duty to act.

- Cassius presents Caesar as a weak and failing leader.

- He uses over-blown language to describe Caesar and contrasts this with a balanced view of Brutus's status.

Reminder

- **Pupils may make other equally creditable points.**

- **Use the performance criteria opposite in conjunction with the exemplar answers to assess the qualities of an answer on a 'best-fit' basis. Weaknesses in one area can be compensated for by strengths in another.**

- **Please refer to page 8 of the Paper 1 mark scheme for guidance on marking the work of pupils who have used an amanuensis or a mechanical aid such as a word processor.**

Fold out this flap for the performance criteria for Task 1.

Julius Caesar Act 1 Scene 2 Task 1				

Marks available	In this scene Cassius seizes the opportunity to talk to Brutus about Caesar.			
U/R 22	**Comment in detail on the different ways Cassius tries to persuade Brutus to think the same way as he does.**			
W/E 16	Before you begin to write you should think about:			
	• why Cassius chooses this moment to speak to Brutus; • the way Cassius uses his understanding of Brutus's character; • the impression of Caesar that Cassius tries to give to Brutus; • the different ways Cassius uses language to persuade Brutus.			

Performance Criteria for UNDERSTANDING AND RESPONSE	Level	Mark
Pupils make a few simple comments about what Cassius says to Brutus about Caesar. They retell parts of the scene and their answers may be only partly relevant. They give references without explanation.	-	2
	below 4	3
	+	4
Pupils make some comments about what Cassius says to Brutus about Caesar with a little explanation. They recognise some of the key features of the scene but may make no reference to persuasion in their answers. They retell or paraphrase some relevant parts of the scene and make references to the text without always linking them to their comments.	-	6
	4	7
	+	8
Pupils give an answer which provides a simple commentary. They offer an overview of the scene showing understanding of some of the ways Cassius tries to persuade Brutus, though their ideas may be undeveloped. Their points are illustrated by references to the text or some words or phrases used by one or more of the characters.	-	10
	5	11
	+	12
Pupils give a reasonably focused answer with some exploration of the text. They offer a detailed commentary on some aspects of the scene showing understanding of the ways Cassius tries to persuade Brutus. They make straightforward comments about the language of one or more of the characters used in the scene, making use of appropriate references to support their ideas.	-	14
	6	15
	+	16
Pupils give a reasonably full answer which shows engagement with the text and a grasp of the task. They give a detailed commentary on the scene, showing understanding of the different ways Cassius tries to persuade Brutus. They recognise how Cassius uses language to give an impression of Caesar and they justify their comments by the use of carefully selected references to the text.	-	18
	7	19
	+	20
Pupils give a confident and sustained answer which shows insight into the presentation of Caesar and how Cassius persuades Brutus to think as he does. Well-selected references are used to illustrate and justify their comments and show appreciation of the impact of language in revealing character and attitude.	above 7	21
		22

Performance Criteria for WRITTEN EXPRESSION	Level	Mark
Some of the pupils' ideas are clearly expressed. The basic grammatical structure of some sentences is correct and some punctuation is used accurately. The spelling of simple words is usually accurate and the handwriting is mostly legible, though there may be obvious weaknesses in the formation of some letters.	- below 4 +	1 2 3
Pupils' ideas are generally clear with some appropriate organisation. Sentence structures and vocabulary are beginning to be used effectively to develop a point of view. Punctuation to mark sentences is mostly used accurately and pupils are beginning to use punctuation within the sentence. The spelling of simple and common polysyllabic words is generally accurate. Handwriting is mostly clear and legible.	- 4 +	4 5 6
Pupils' writing is clearly expressed and usually organised into a straightforward structure or paragraphs. Vocabulary and sentence structures are sometimes chosen effectively to clarify and develop their point of view, but may not be maintained convincingly throughout. A range of punctuation, including commas, apostrophes and quotation marks, is usually used accurately. Spelling, including that of words with complex regular patterns, is usually accurate. Handwriting is generally clear and legible in a fluent style.	- 5 +	7 8 9
Pupils' writing is clear, structured and mostly in an appropriate style for a discursive piece. The use of vocabulary and grammatical structures, together with appropriate paragraphing, contribute to the clarity of the writing, though the same quality may not be evident throughout. A range of punctuation is usually used correctly to clarify meaning. Spelling is accurate, though there may be some errors in difficult words. Handwriting is in a fluent and legible style.	- 6 +	10 11 12
Pupils' writing is confident and organised, and it is in an appropriate style, although it may be unsophisticated in tone at times. Ideas are developed by a range of grammatical features and the effective use of vocabulary. Paragraphing and punctuation are used to make the sequence of ideas clear. Spelling, including that of complex irregular words, is correct. Handwriting is in a fluent and legible style.	- 7 +	13 14 15
Pupils' writing presents arguments clearly in a coherent way. The choice of style and structure, supported by the precise use of vocabulary and grammatical structures, enables clarity and emphasis to be achieved. Pupils show a consistent grasp of the correct use of paragraphing and a range of punctuation. Spelling, including that of complex irregular words, is correct. Handwriting is in a fluent and legible style.	above 7	16

Example 4

Julius Caesar, Act 4 Scene 3, Task 2.

I know this is a turning point, for Rome and for me but my wife portia has died and I feel as if life could not go on. I would like to forget her ~~but~~ but something in my mind tells me not to. I try to bury my feelings with wine ~~it~~ but that makes me unhappy still but I will not show ~~my~~ feelings to anyone The conversation with cassius was all about just fighting thats all it ever is but still we have to go on ~~the enemy~~ at phillipi we will face ~~them~~ him our legions are brimful our cause is ripe but the deep of night is crept on I will go to sleep but why why did that ghost appear ive no idea he called me an evil spirit the ghost itself told me that ~~to~~ I shall meet him at philippi then ~~somehow~~ just it vanished now the battle of

Philippi is coming up I, I don't know what ~~to~~ ~~we~~ I should do we will do good I know it, but what if we don't, what if we don't win then what should I do but don't think like that We will do good ~~ant~~ we will march up there this will be the voyage of thy life And we must take the current when it serves. Or lose our ventures. we will go on. we'll along our selves and meet them at pillippi. Early tommorrow we will rise e hence.

Example 4

UNDERSTANDING AND RESPONSE

The pupil understands the requirements of the task and gives a clear, if undeveloped, response. There are relevant, straightforward comments about Brutus's feelings with a little explanation: 'my wife portia has died and I feel as if life could not go on'. The pupil conveys something of Brutus's confusion and often introduces quotations quite effectively, but finds it difficult to sustain the role and lapses into narrative and paraphrase at the end. Such a response merits a mark at the top of the Level 4 band.

Key Considerations

- straightforward comments about Brutus's feelings;
- a little explanation;
- attempts to assume the role.

Level: 4+   *Mark: 8*

WRITTEN EXPRESSION

The response is reasonably clearly expressed and organised though there is no attempt at paragraphing. Initially there is some control over sentence structure, but this deteriorates and as the answer proceeds, sentence demarcation becomes less secure. Together with no effective use of internal sentence punctuation, this leads to a lack of clarity of meaning. There is an attempt to write in Brutus's voice ('this will be the voyage of thy life') and to integrate quotation ('Early tommorrow we will rise & hence'). Spelling is usually accurate, but with lapses such as 'tommorrow'. The response gives evidence of Level 4 performance.

Key Considerations

- reasonably clear;
- generally accurate spelling;
- weak punctuation.

Level: 4-   *Mark: 4*

Example 5

Julius Caesar, Act 4 Scene 3, Task 2.

I know this is a turning point, for Rome and for me. I do not know what the future may be. We may not win the battle of Philippi, but we will try. We must attack soon otherwise the army will grow tired of waiting. The enemy are strong and are getting stronger every day we wait. If we were to attack tomorrow, or soon after we would have a much easier fight. I am deeply saddened by my wifes death but this shouldn't affect me, it can't affect me, I have a whole army to lead into a battle. Caesers ghost appeared and said we would meet at Philippi This could mean that we will meet again, that I will die. Cassius and I have fought. I hate it when we fight but I feel so guilty over Caesers death, and I sometimes think he did the dreadful deed because of his jelousy for Caesor. He thought we should wait and let the enemy find us to have a battle. I think it is a silly idea, even though the enemy would be tired after searching, they would have gathered more men and soldiers on the way. If we left tomorrow we could

gather the people from the town
and villages that are on the journey
I have lead a very healthy and rich life,
but it soon came to an end at once I killed
Caeser. He was my best friend. He was
also a leader, a single leader, too powerful to
understand. Now Octavius and Mark Anthony
are to kill me. I have decided, we shall fight
as soon as possible. I must rest and try
to get rid of my troubles. Good reason must
of force give place to better. The people twixt Philippi
and this ground Do stand but in a forced affection.
From which advantage shall we cut him off.
If at Philippi we do face him there, these
people at our back.

Example 5

UNDERSTANDING AND RESPONSE

This pupil has produced a reasonably focused answer which maintains the voice of Brutus ('I am deeply saddened by my wifes death'; 'I must rest and try to get rid of my troubles'). There is understanding of the differences between Brutus and Cassius on tactical issues, of Brutus's personal situation and feelings, and the role is well maintained. However, despite good use of reference, these points are not explored in great detail and chances to comment on the way characters speak are missed as in the undeveloped quotations at the end. Hence, some of the qualities required for Level 6 are present, but only sufficiently so to warrant a mark at the bottom of the Level 6 band.

Key Considerations

* good focus on Brutus, his views and his situation;
* detailed reference to scene;
* points not explored in much detail.

Level: 6-   *Mark: 14*

WRITTEN EXPRESSION

This writing is clear and well organised. A consistent voice is adopted for Brutus, supported by appropriate vocabulary and grammatical structures, although there are some slight lapses, for example, 'I think it is a silly idea'. There are no paragraphs, but punctuation apart from apostrophes is usually accurate. Spelling is accurate and handwriting is legible and a mark in the Level 6 range is appropriate.

Key Considerations

* clear structure and appropriate style;
* no paragraphing, but generally technically accurate;
* effective voice.

Level: 6-   *Mark: 10*

Example 6

Julius Caesar, Act 4 Scene 3, Task 2.

I know this a turning point for Rome and for me because of everything that has happened to me recently, the arguement with Cassius the death of my wife Portia and most of all the sight of Cuesars ghost. It has been a hard time for me.

I couldn't believe it when I heard of Portia's death. I felt she was impatient of my absence and feared the power of Octarcius and Antony's army. She was a brave wife and person to die in such a way of swallowing fire. I found it very difficult to tell Cassius but because he was such a close friend it made it easier. I had to put on a brave face though because there was a very important day coming up, So I drowned my sorraws with a bowl of wine. Cassius continued to comfort me by saying "I ~~couldn't~~ cannot drink to much of Brutus' love"

Cassius has been very kind to me recently apart from our last arguement. Cassius and I always seem to be arguing over the simplist of things which we never agree on. This time it was whether we should march to philipi or not. It was obvious that we should. We had the army at its peak, ready to fight, and as Antony's army was increasing by the day I felt it was right to march to Philipi and catch them off guard. Of course Cassius had completely the opposite idea. He said "Tis better the enemy seek us," I have to admit it was a good point but my one was better. Cassius took the loss of the arguement all in his stride. He has learnt to, and as we are such close friends, I don't think he minds.

The evening of the arguement the strangest thing happened to me. I had just invited my Servanto into my tent to sleep, and Lucius has just fallen asleep after playing a little music to me when Caesar's ghost appeared. I was speechless as well as breathless, I just couldn't believe what I was seeing.

To begin with I couldn't see anyone but I knew someone was there because I noticed the candle flickering. I asked who was there and he answered "They evil spirit, Brutus" I looked around and saw Caesars ghost. I asked why he was here, he replied "thou shalt see me at Philipi" He then repeated himself and left I quickly found my slaves and asked them if they had seen anything, they just said in turn. "No."

I asked them to go and ge Cassius, so I could explain what had happened I was still puzzled by what had happened t the ghost had said "thou shalt see me at Philipi" did it mean something? I wasn't sure.

Example 6

UNDERSTANDING AND RESPONSE

The pupil has focused well on Brutus's mixed feelings throughout the response. References are aptly selected and carefully integrated into the monologue and there is an implicit awareness of how the use of language contributes to the atmosphere and tension in the detail of the 'candle flickering' and the repetition of the ghost's 'thou shalt see me at Philipi'. The pupil's remarks about Cassius's response to the news of Portia's death reveal a good understanding of Brutus's insight into the character of Cassius – so too do the reflections on their argument: 'Cassius took the loss of the arguement all in his stride'. The final paragraph effectively communicates Brutus's uncertainty about the significance of the ghost. Overall, this piece is evidence of Level 7 performance.

Key Considerations

- role of Brutus convincingly sustained;
- commentary closely linked to the text with good use of quotation;
- insight into Brutus's feelings and reactions to events of the scene;
- implied awareness of the contribution of language to mood and atmosphere.

Level: 7   Mark: 19

WRITTEN EXPRESSION

The response is well organised and sustains an appropriate tone throughout. Paragraphing and punctuation are confidently used to sequence the monologue. A range of vocabulary and sentence structures are used. 'I drowned my sorrows with a bowl of wine' and 'I was speechless as well as breathless' indicate the pupil's ability to imply Brutus's reactions to the events he is recounting. Spelling is sound and handwriting clear and legible. The piece has been given a mark in the middle of the Level 7 range.

Key Considerations

- appropriate tone well sustained;
- material well organised and clearly presented.

Level: 7   Mark: 14

> **Reward fully answers which provide either explicitly or implicitly an explanation of Brutus's reactions to his situation and which focus on his thoughts as well as his feelings.**
>
> **Keep looking for evidence of positive achievement and, if you think an answer clearly deserves a particular level, place it securely into that level.**

Content

Pupils may refer to some of the following points in their answers. These points do not imply that there is a required content. Pupils may include and develop some of these points, but not necessarily all of them or in this order.

- Brutus's inner feelings about Portia's death and how these may contrast with his apparent philosophic acceptance of her death.

- Brutus's insistence that his battle plans are better than Cassius's and his reconciliation with Cassius.

- Brutus's anxiety about the provenance of the ghost and its purpose.

- Brutus's loneliness before the battle.

Reminder

- **Pupils may make other equally creditable points.**

- **Use the performance criteria opposite in conjunction with the exemplar answers to assess the qualities of an answer on a 'best-fit' basis. Weaknesses in one area can be compensated for by strengths in another.**

- **Please refer to page 8 of the Paper 1 mark scheme for guidance on marking the work of pupils who have used an amanuensis or a mechanical aid such as a word processor.**

Fold out this flap for the performance criteria for Task 2.

Julius Caesar Act 4 Scene 3 Task 2

Marks available	This scene takes place before the battle of Philippi and after the quarrel with Cassius.
U/R 22	**Imagine you are Brutus. Write down and explain your thoughts and feelings at this tense and difficult time.**
W/E 16	You could begin: *I know this is a turning point for Rome and for me ...*
	Before you begin to write you should decide what Brutus thought and felt about:
	• the death of his wife, Portia; • his conversations with Cassius; • why the ghost appeared; • the battle of Philippi that was soon going to take place.

Performance Criteria for UNDERSTANDING AND RESPONSE	Level	Mark
Pupils retell a few events in this scene, mainly from Brutus's point of view. They include sections of the scene without comment, offering simple opinions about the main events. Pupils may slip out of role and write about Brutus in the third person.	- below 4 +	2 3 4
Pupils adopt the role of Brutus but may struggle to maintain it throughout the whole of their answer. They make a few comments about his feelings or views on the other characters or events with a little explanation. They retell or paraphrase some relevant parts of the scene and make references to the text without always linking them to their comments.	- 4 +	6 7 8
Pupils give an answer that provides a simple commentary, mostly from Brutus's point of view. They offer an overview of Brutus's character and his thoughts and feelings at this time, although their ideas may be undeveloped. Their points are illustrated by references to the text or some words or phrases used by Brutus that suggest the tension and difficulties he is experiencing.	- 5 +	10 11 12
Pupils give a reasonably focused answer which shows some understanding of Brutus's character, his confusion and the strength of his feelings. They successfully maintain the role of Brutus and there is detailed reference to parts of the scene, exploring his thoughts about the tensions and difficulties he is experiencing. Pupils show some awareness of the effects of the way the characters speak to each other in the scene.	- 6 +	14 15 16
Pupils give a reasonably full answer, focusing on Brutus's thoughts and feelings and maintaining the role of Brutus convincingly. They give a detailed commentary on the scene which is closely linked to the text and shows an insight into Brutus's view of his situation and the mixed nature of his feelings. Pupils make appropriate reference to the text and show understanding of the way the tension in the scene is increased by the way the characters speak to each other.	- 7 +	18 19 20
Pupils sustain the role of Brutus convincingly in a confident answer which shows insight into his character and the complexities and subtleties of his view of his situation. Well-selected references are used to develop their answers and show appreciation of the impact of language in revealing character and attitude.	above 7	21 22

Be generous in the interpretation of what constitutes an appropriate style and form for this empathetic task. Remember that aspects of the character's role and opinions are assessed within the criteria for Understanding and Response. The focus in Written Expression should be on how accurately and effectively the pupils maintain their chosen style.

Performance Criteria for WRITTEN EXPRESSION	Level	Mark
Some of the pupils' ideas are clearly expressed. There is a limited attempt to use the chosen voice for the character. The basic grammatical structure of some sentences is correct and some punctuation is used accurately. The spelling of simple words is usually accurate and the handwriting is mostly legible though there may be obvious weaknesses in the formation of some letters.	- below 4 +	1 2 3
Pupils' ideas are generally clear with some appropriate organisation. Sentence structures and vocabulary are beginning to be used to develop a voice for the character but this may not be consistently achieved. Punctuation to mark sentences is mostly used accurately and pupils are beginning to use punctuation within the sentence. The spelling of simple and common polysyllabic words is generally accurate. Handwriting is mostly clear and legible.	- 4 +	4 5 6
Pupils' writing is clearly expressed and usually organised into a straightforward structure or paragraphs. Vocabulary and sentence structures are sometimes chosen effectively to create an appropriate voice for the character but may not be maintained convincingly throughout. A range of punctuation, including commas, apostrophes and quotation marks, is usually used accurately. Spelling, including that of words with complex regular patterns, is usually accurate. Handwriting is generally clear and legible in a fluent style.	- 5 +	7 8 9
Pupils' writing is clear, structured and mostly in an appropriate style and tone for the character. The use of vocabulary and grammatical structures contributes to an appropriate tone for the voice though the same quality may not be evident throughout. A range of punctuation and paragraphing is usually used correctly to clarify meaning. Spelling is accurate though there may be some errors in difficult words. Handwriting is in a fluent and legible style.	- 6 +	10 11 12
Pupils' writing is confident, organised and written in an appropriate style for the character, although it may be unconvincing in tone at times. The grammatical features and choice of vocabulary are appropriate for the character and contribute to the effect of the piece. Paragraphing and punctuation are used correctly to make the sequence of thoughts and feelings clear. Spelling, including that of complex irregular words, is correct. Handwriting is in a fluent and legible style.	- 7 +	13 14 15
Pupils' writing is coherent and written with distinctive structural or stylistic effects appropriate to the chosen voice for the character. The precise use of vocabulary and grammatical structures enables clarity and emphasis to be achieved. Pupils show a consistent grasp of the correct use of paragraphing and a range of punctuation. Spelling, including that of complex irregular words, is correct. Handwriting is in a fluent and legible style.	above 7	16

Example 7

A Midsummer Night's Dream, Act 2 Scene 1, Task 3.

Oberon is the King of the fairy Kingdom and he has a Queen called Titania. Oberon has a sevent called Puck and Titania has the fairy.

Oberon is a selfish King who thinks that everything he wants should be done, without an argument from anyone including his Queen Titania.

Oberon wants a baby boy from Titania to serve him and to be the next king of the fairy Kingdom but Titania will not give him the boy that he wants so Oberon gets very angry with Titania. Oberon orders Puck his servent to go and get a magic flower so when you fall asleep the juice of this magic flower is dripped onto your eyelids so when you awake you will fall madly inlove with the first living creature you see.

When Puck returns to the land of the fairy Kingdom he is ordered by oberon to drip the juice of the magic flower on Oberon's Queen Titania in the hope she will fall inlove with a beast.

122

Queen Titania will not give Oberon, the baby he wants, as many people in this day and age having died while giving birth to their children so Titania is scared for her life, she thinks Oberon is selfish and should not be given everything he wants.

Puck is a naughty little fairy who does not like humans and think that they are stupid. Puck likes to play tricks on humans and make them do stupid things.

Puck is Oberon's servant and does every thing he is told. When Puck is ordered by King Oberon to go and get a magic flower from a distant land he comes back and sees some humans in the forest. These human are in love. There are four of them so he decides to play a little trick on them. When two of them are asleep he put the juice of the magic flower onto the eyelids of the males. He is woken by the other two humans who are chasing after them and

the human with the magic on his
eyelids awakes and sees the
other female and falls inlove with
her. Puck does the same to the
other male when he is asleep
so when he awakes he will fall in
love with the same girl as the other
one did.

Puck goes and tells Oberon and
Puck and Oberon have a laugh
about it, but Puck still had
not done, what he set out to
do. Puck finds Queen Titaria when
she is sleeping and drips the
juice of the magic flower onto
Titaria's eye lids so when she
awakes she hopefully falls in
love with a beast like a lion,
bear, wolf or a bull.

If I was going to create an
atmosphere in this play I would
focus on way the fairys use
their magic to hide from humans
any play trick on humans and
on their own kind in the
fairy kingdom.

Example 7

UNDERSTANDING AND RESPONSE

This pupil takes a narrative approach, which does not fully address the question but shows some understanding of the scene. There are occasional comments about what happens with a little explanation ('Oberon is a selfish king who thinks ...'; 'Puck likes to play tricks'). Only in the last paragraph is there an attempt to offer advice, as a director might, on creating atmosphere and mood. Therefore, a mark in the middle of the Level 4 range has been awarded.

Key Considerations

* struggles to write as director;
* comments about fairy world.

Level: 4   Mark: 7

WRITTEN EXPRESSION

This piece is clearly organised using paragraphs and generally accurate punctuation, both to mark sentences and within them. Vocabulary and sentence structures generally convey meaning clearly although there is no attempt to give emphasis to specific points. Spelling is usually accurate and handwriting is fairly clear and legible in a fluent style. The pupil's written expression therefore merits a mark in the Level 5 range.

Key Considerations

* clear organisation;
* some effective sentence structures and vocabulary.

Level: 5   Mark: 8

Example 8

A Midsummer Night's Dream, Act 2 Scene 1, Task 3.

The fairies part would play ~~their part~~ in a joyful way and would do everything their master said. For titania's fairies you would have to nice, kind and loving because titania is like that heself, they would have to follow ~~it~~ what she said and do it. The main thing don't like oberon unless titania likes him. Titania's fairies do good things like put the dew into the flower in the morning or hang a pearl in every cowslip's ear. You would have to be stubern as well because of oberon trying to get the boy and the fairies would have to stand by their master which is titania. The atmosphere to titania's fairies would be peceful colourful and ~~smell~~ sweetly and the fairies would sing when they wanted to, ~~to~~ sing titania to sleep with the boy, would be good. The effects I would use to creat the fairy world would be light colours everywhere and flower and a little sprkerling ~~pearl~~ strem going right through the middle of the stage. Birds singing in trees and bunny's and animals like that as well. The audience hopefully would fill relex in this part of the fairy kingdom.

Oberon's ~~fairy~~ puck is horrible he plays tricks on human and he thinks it funny and he is a jester to oberon because ~~of~~ all the things he does which makes oberon laugh. I think puck is trying to be more like oberon and do horrible things like him. In his part of the fairy kingdom it will be dark not a lot of life about and just a pond ~~fau~~ of durty water. The person playing puck would have to be horrible, naughty igorent and spiltful abit arity to. Puck would have to do all that oberon tells him to do otherwise oberon will hert him or put a spell on him so he does ~~what~~ he is told. The atmosphere wouldn't be very nice either horrible to live in nothing grow no-one happy and joyful nothing like that it would be like a dungon. The effect for this part of the fairy kingdom would be some time rain, mud, little bit of grass lots of tress so they can hide and scare people as they are walking past. So really quite the opposite of Titania's part of the woods. The audience would fill cold and frightened in this part of the woods and may be abit when weary because wouldn't now what was going to happern next. When oberon ask's puck to get the flower because titania won't give him the boy the he wants so much. This flower would make titania fall in love with the first living thing she sees even if it is a lion, bear, or wolf, or bull or even a maddling monkey, or a busy ape, it could hurt her but he doesn't care just so he can get the boy to be his henchman to serve him. In this part of the story the weather doesn't know what it's doing because they (titania and oberon) are argumer arguing and so the kingdom doesn't know if it's winter, spring, summer or Autumn So the fairies would have do lots of thing for each season, all at once.

Example 8

UNDERSTANDING AND RESPONSE

This pupil gives a simple commentary on the fairies and their world, focusing on the atmosphere of the scene. There is an awareness of the contrast between the atmosphere engendered by Titania and that created by Oberon and Puck and a consideration of the effects which could be used to create the atmosphere, though the ideas are fairly generalised and not tied closely to the text (for example, 'The atmosphere to titania's fairies would be peceful colourful and smell sweetly'). There are general comments on the character and role of Puck and some speculation ('I think puck is trying to be more like oberon') but this is not supported by reference to the text. This response can be best described by the Level 5 performance criteria.

Key Considerations

* simple, generalised commentary;
* consideration of atmosphere;
* lack of close reference.

Level: 5   Mark: 11

WRITTEN EXPRESSION

The response is usually clearly expressed and reasonably well organised, but there is no consistent use of paragraphs. The pupil tries to write as a director in the first few lines, but has difficulty in sustaining it: for example, 'The main thing don't like Oberon'. Punctuation between sentences is generally accurate, but within sentences it is variable and use of the apostrophe is erratic: 'light colour's everywhere'; 'Birds singing in tree's'. Capital letters are not always used appropriately. Spelling of simple words is usually accurate, despite errors in some common words: 'spiltful' for 'spiteful', 'fill' for 'feel' and 'now' for 'know'. The piece is therefore given a mark at the bottom of the Level 5 range.

Key Considerations

* reasonably clearly expressed and organised;
* difficulty in sustaining the voice;
* spelling errors in common words.

Level: 5-   Mark: 7

Example 9

A Midsummer Night's Dream, Act 2 Scene 1, Task 3.

1) When I audition for the cast and I come to the fairy world I would want the pupils to be able to show how magical their world is. When they speak they should not speak like every day people or even the people set in this play. You should be able to watch the play and realize who they are. At the start of Act 2 scene 1 Fairy speaks, she is using rhythming couplets "Over hill, over dale

Thorough bush, thorough briar,
Over Park, over pale
Thorough flood, thorough fire "

(2-5) This is one way to realize how different she is to other people. I would expect her to be quite small, ~~and~~ thin and tiny and to have a light squeaky voice, but one you can hear. She should use her hands to describe things when she speaks. There is an atmospere of love and magical powers so the pupil playing her should express this when she is acting by her tone of voice. or her hand movements

Reading through the scene I can tell Puck ~~is~~ is mischeveous and sneaky.

You can tell this by what fairy says "Or else you are that shrewd and knavish sprite" (33) "I am that merry wanderer of the night" (43)

You can tell that he likes being the character he is. So I would tell the pupil playing Puck that he should be rather pleased and jolly, but also with a nasty side to him, so he could maybe a walk around with his back bent or to over a bit and have a wierd ~~suspicious~~ smile on his face. (When he speaks he should speak with maybe a croaky voice to and make it noticable, maybe a bit scarey, to make the audience know that he is not a very nice character.

Oberon is the king of fairy land. He is a very respected person everyone seems to look up to him and obey him. Puck describes him as the strong leader before he enters the scene. The only person who does not obey him is his wife ~~Titania~~ Titania, the queen. They have fallen out and when they speak to each other things go really bad in the fairy world. Puck describes how scared all the fairies are.

"that all their elves for fear.
Creep into acorn cups and hide
them there" (30-31) The These
two people, Oberon and Titania are very
powerful people. I would want the
pupils playing them both to be very strong
and hard people who don't let anyone let
them beat them. I would ask the
pupil playing Oberon to stand tall all
the time and never put his head down.
He would need to have a very deep
voice and would not smile, he would have
to act very serious and mean every
word he was saying. - Titania would
be a strong women. She would also need
to stand tall and have a serious voice.
I think she could smile a little though
to show she is a women but not when
she is around Oberon, she needs to show
how tough she is and that he cannot
tell her what to do. When Oberon and
Titania are together they need to
be so very serious and look at each
other right into the eyes and speak
very loudly and deeply to make the
audience sense the negativity between
them both.
       The atmosphere is very important.
I would need to have the scenery

132

of trees and flowers because the scene is set in the woods. You could have bird noises playing in the background to show the nature of the wood and fairyland.

Bright coloured lights would be good to show the magical power. You could shine a white light at fairy and puck and when Oberon and Titania come in you could shine a red light to show ~~the anger of them both~~ their anger.

Example 9

UNDERSTANDING AND RESPONSE

This response shows that the pupil has focused well on the task; at every stage of the answer a director's perspective has been adopted. Although in the earlier part some of the ideas are rather vague and need more supporting reference, the presentation of the characters is discussed, with suggestions about how they could be acted, together with ideas for effective and appropriate lighting to emphasise their mood. Understanding of the character of Puck is revealed through the analysis of his conversation with the other fairy; the relationship between Oberon and Titania is also clearly described. There is some relevant quotation, though this is not always very well integrated into the speech of the director. The impact of language is (apart from the mistaken identification of rhyming couplets) implied to some extent through comments on the way in which individual characters might speak. This piece has been given a mark in the middle of the Level 6 band.

Key Considerations

- discussion of how characters might be presented;
- some focus on mood and atmosphere;
- limited awareness of the impact of language, even implicit.

Level: 6   *Mark: 15*

WRITTEN EXPRESSION

The writing is clear and well organised into paragraphs. The style and tone is well adapted to conveying the sort of advice and instructions a director might give. Vocabulary is sometimes effectively and precisely used; for example, Puck is 'mischeveous and sneaky' and the audience senses the 'negativity' between Oberon and Titania, but at other times is rather vague: 'he is not a very nice character'; Titania 'could smile a little though to show she is a women'. Spelling and punctuation are accurate, and handwriting fluent and legible. This pupil's written expression therefore merits a mark in the Level 6 band.

Key Considerations

- vocabulary effectively used to describe characters;
- awareness of the appropriate tone and style for a director.

Level: 6   *Mark: 11*

Example 10

A Midsummer Night's Dream, Act 2 Scene 1, Task 3.

Pupils playing oberon :-
Oberon has a big, demanding part for the play. The actor is to play it with full feeling, and use all their acting skills. Oberon really wants the Indian boy from Titania, but Titania is using all her powers to stop him.
Oberon should pressurise Titania, after all he is her husband, as in line 63.
"Tarry, rash wanton! Am not I thy lord?"
This line should be delivered with a loud, demanding voice, full of power and authority. The same applies for line 118 - 120.
"Do you amend it, then it lies in you.
Why should Titania cross her Oberon?
I do but beg a little changeling boy
To be my henchman."
The lines should be read with ~~rhyth~~ rhythm, but not rhymed. Sentences should be structured. (Blank verse).
For lines 74 - 80, Titania is accusing Oberon of loving Hippolyta. Oberon replies,
"How canst thou thus, for shame, Titania,
Glance at my credit with Hippolyta,
Knowing I know thy love to Theseus?

Didst not thou lead him through
the glimmering night
From Perigenia, whom he ravished,
And make him with fair Aegles break his
faith
With Ariadne, and Antiopa?"
These lines should be delivered less
fiercely, with a hint of scarcasm for
Oberon is trying to make Titania see
he's not going to take talk like that
from her.
By the end of the play the audience
should be loathing Oberon for the way
he treats and conquers his wife. And if
by the end of our play they do we
know the actor has played his part correctly.
  Pupil playing Titania:-
  Again this part should be played with
full feeling, you should stand up for your
self and answer oberon with full
confidence. Argue your lines with Oberon.
As in line 61, say lines with confidence-
don't let Oberon overpower you on stage.
  "What, jealous Oberon? Fairies, skip hence
  I have forsworn his bed and company."
Again in lines 64 - 68 answer Oberon
back, deliver lines which have meanings-
you want to keep your Indian boy.
  "Then I must be thy lady. But I know

when thou hast stol'n away from
Fairyland,
And in the shape of Corin sat all day
Playing on pipes of corn, and versing love
To amorous Phillida."
Oberon is trying to steal your boy, the
boy your best friend dyed giving birth
to. Deliver lines 122 - 137 with a feeling
of sadness and remorse, showing Oberon
you'll never give him up.
By the end of the play the audience
should feel very unhappy for Titania,
delivering lines as directed should bring
the sadness out of the audience.
Pupil playing Puck:-
Puck offers a little bit of happiness
and humour for the audience. All of Puck's
lines a rhyming cuplets (strong ryhthm &
last words of lines ryhme.) Emphasise the
fact they rhyme, boast and be happy of
the things you do. As in lines 42 - 44.
"Thou speakest aright;
I am that merry wanderer of the night.
I jest to Oberon, and make him smile "
And in lines 51 - 53, be proud off what
you have done.
"The wisest aunt, telling the saddest tale,
Sometime for threefoot stool mistaketh me;

Then &slip I from her bum, down topples she,

And 'Tailor' cries, and falls into a cough."

By the end of the play the audience should like Puck for the humour he adds to the play, and the mischeviousness he brings into it.

The effects the play shall have are :-

1). Props to be made larger than the pupil - adding to the affect of tinyness).

2). Stage will be dusky and smoky - this adds to the affect of un-reality and the world of the fairies.

3). Costumes of the actors shall look to ~~Be~~ be made out of things of nature such as :- mouse skins, spiders webs, leaves, flower petals e.t.c. This is to show tinyness & daintyness of the fairies in M.S.N Dream.

If all lines are delivered with full feeling as directed and all the affects added it should create a successful atmosphere. The costumes, tinyness of the actors compaired to props and the smoky stage should give the audience a sense of magic and confuse them of what's reality and what isn't.

The scene between Oberon, Titania, Puck and the Indian boys has great importance and is an interesting part of the play to cover. Things which happen in this scene can affect the storyline and ending of the play. All actors should play this part to the greatest of their ability to and really show how important it is.

Example 10

UNDERSTANDING AND RESPONSE

The role of the director is embedded in every line of this response, and the pupil conveys successfully the importance of seeing this scene in a theatrical context ('The costumes, tinyness of the actors compaired to props and the smoky stage should give the audience a sense of magic'). Characterisation, audience response, props – all these are dealt with, and evidence from the text is always produced to support the argument. There is a strong emphasis on language, and a keen awareness of the impact of Shakespeare's verse. The vigorous approach adopted by the pupil conveys a strong personal response, and such qualities are best described by a mark above Level 7.

Key Considerations

- keen awareness of the role of the director;
- strong sense of the theatrical potential of the scene;
- good emphasis on language, with appropriate textual reference.

Level: 7+   Mark: 20

WRITTEN EXPRESSION

The ideas of a director are clearly and convincingly expressed in this piece of writing. Carefully chosen vocabulary is used to define the key features of the characters ('demanding', 'pressurise', 'mischeviousness', 'loathing'); the response is well structured and effectively paragraphed. Occasionally, over-ambitious sentences are attempted and they become scrambled, but the general impression is of a pupil who has a strong grasp of syntax, and the confidence to convey a clear view of how the scene should be staged with a tone of knowledgeable authority. Overall, then, a mark in the middle of the Level 7 range is appropriate.

Key Considerations

- vocabulary used effectively to define characters;
- strong sense of the appropriate tone and style for the director.

Level: 7   Mark: 14

Some pupils will base their answers on a study of the text of this scene while others may focus in detail on a performance. The performance criteria can apply to both these approaches and both should be given equal credit.

Keep looking for evidence of positive achievement and if you think an answer clearly deserves a particular level, place it securely into that level.

Content

Pupils may refer to some of the following points in their answers. These points do not imply that there is a required content. Pupils may include and develop some of these points, but not necessarily all of them or in this order.

- Oberon is 'jealous' and Titania is 'proud'. They have great influence in the fairy and the human worlds. This should be suggested by their actions and what they say.

- Puck's mischievousness should be emphasised in the actor's performance.

- The set, costumes and performances should illustrate the magical and anarchic world of the fairies.

- Music and lighting could be used effectively to create the magical and ethereal world of the fairies.

Reminder

- Pupils may make other equally creditable points.

- Use the performance criteria opposite in conjunction with the exemplar answers to assess the qualities of an answer on a 'best-fit' basis. Weaknesses in one area can be compensated for by strengths in another.

- Please refer to page 8 of the Paper 1 mark scheme for guidance on marking the work of pupils who have used an amanuensis or a mechanical aid such as a word processor.

Fold out this flap for the performance criteria for Task 3.

A Midsummer Night's Dream Act 2 Scene 1 Task 3

Marks available	Imagine you are going to direct this scene for your year group.
U/R 22	**Explain how you want the fairies to play their parts and what you want to suggest to the audience about the fairy world.**
W/E 16	Before you begin to write you should think about:
	• what you would tell the pupils playing Oberon and Titania about how to play their parts;
	• what you would say to the pupil playing Puck about his role;
	• the atmosphere you want to create and how you would do this;
	• the effects you would use to create the fairy world.

Performance Criteria for UNDERSTANDING AND RESPONSE	Level	Mark
Pupils make a few simple comments about the fairies or their world in this scene. They retell parts of the scene and their answers may be only partly relevant. They give references without explanation and may not write as a director.	-	2
	below 4	3
	+	4
Pupils make some comments about the fairies or their world with a little explanation, but they may struggle to write as a director. They retell or paraphrase some relevant parts of the scene and make references without always linking them to their comments.	-	6
	4	7
	+	8
Pupils give an answer that provides a simple commentary on the fairies and their world. They begin to comment on the atmosphere they want to create as a director and identify some of the effects they would use to do this. Their points are illustrated by references to the text or some words and phrases used by one or more of the characters.	-	10
	5	11
	+	12
Pupils give a reasonably focused answer with some exploration of the text. They offer a detailed commentary on some aspects of the scene, showing understanding of the fairies and their world and how this might be created on stage. They make straightforward comments about the language of one or more of the characters in the scene, showing an awareness of how this adds to the impression the audience gains of the fairy world. Pupils make use of appropriate reference to the text to support their ideas.	-	14
	6	15
	+	16
Pupils give a reasonably full answer which is closely linked to the text and shows a grasp of the task. They give detailed advice on the interpretation of the role of the fairies and their world in a commentary that shows understanding of the use of language and its contribution to the effects of this scene on the audience. Pupils justify their comments by the use of carefully selected references to the text.	-	18
	7	19
	+	20
Pupils give a confident and sustained answer which shows insight into the fairies and their world. The full and detailed advice on direction shows an ability to appreciate the impact of language and atmosphere in this scene and the effect they have on the audience. Well-selected references are used to illustrate and justify their comments.	above 7	21
		22

Be generous in the interpretation of what constitutes an appropriate style and form to express a director's opinions. Remember the director's views, advice, etc. are assessed within the criteria for Understanding and Response.

Pupils may, for example, adopt an informal style in explaining their ideas which is acceptable. They may also make repeated use of the same form of sentence structure, using the conditional, 'I would'.

Performance Criteria for WRITTEN EXPRESSION	Level	Mark
Some of the pupils' ideas are clearly expressed. The basic grammatical structure of some sentences is correct and some punctuation is used accurately. The spelling of simple words is usually accurate and the handwriting is mostly legible, though there may be obvious weaknesses in the formation of some letters.	- below 4 +	1 2 3
Pupils' ideas are generally clear with some appropriate organisation. Sentence structures and vocabulary are beginning to be used to convey advice effectively but this may not be consistently maintained. Punctuation to mark sentences is mostly used accurately and pupils are beginning to use punctuation within the sentence. The spelling of simple and common polysyllabic words is generally accurate. Handwriting is mostly clear and legible.	- 4 +	4 5 6
Pupils' writing is clearly expressed and usually organised into a straightforward structure or paragraphs. Vocabulary and sentence structures are sometimes chosen effectively to convey advice, but may not be maintained convincingly throughout. A range of punctuation, including commas, apostrophes and quotation marks, is usually used accurately. Spelling, including that of words with complex regular patterns, is usually accurate. Handwriting is generally clear and legible in a fluent style.	- 5 +	7 8 9
Pupils' writing is clear, structured and mostly in an appropriate style and tone for conveying advice, although there may be lapses. The use of vocabulary and grammatical structures together with appropriate paragraphing contribute to the clarity of the writing, though the same quality may not be evident throughout. A range of punctuation is usually used correctly to clarify meaning. Spelling is accurate though there may be some errors in difficult words. Handwriting is in a fluent and legible style.	- 6 +	10 11 12
Pupils' writing is confident, organised and written in an appropriate style for conveying advice, although it may be unsophisticated in tone at times. The grammatical features and choice of vocabulary contribute to the clarity of the piece. Paragraphing and punctuation are used correctly to make the sequence of thoughts and feelings clear. Spelling, including that of complex irregular words, is correct. Handwriting is in a fluent and legible style.	- 7 +	13 14 15
The pupils' writing presents the director's ideas in a coherent way. The choice of style and structure, supported by the precise use of vocabulary and grammatical structures, enables clarity and emphasis to be achieved. Pupils show a consistent grasp of the correct use of paragraphing and a range of punctuation. Spelling, including that of complex irregular words, is correct. Handwriting is in a fluent and legible style.	above 7	16

Example 11

A Midsummer Night's Dream, Act 3 Scene 2, Task 4.

> I'm so confused, there must be a curse on me because ~~my love~~ Lysander & Demetrius are bieng unkind. They tell me that they love me and are fighting over me. I wish they would both go away. And guase what, even Hermia is in on the joke just to spite me. They call all sorts of names. But i've had enough so im going Athens, So they can leave me alone. "Bye".

Example 11

UNDERSTANDING AND RESPONSE

This is a very short response which at least illustrates some awareness of the main features of the scene, viewed from Helena's perspective. Her indignation at Hermia's apparent betrayal of her is communicated, as is her sense of confusion ('there must be a curse on me'). The first person voice is sustained. No analysis of character or motivation is offered in response to the prompts in the task, and so this piece is placed in the range below Level 4.

Key Considerations

- limited scope of the response;
- basic awareness of Helena's predicament.

Level: below 4   *Mark: 3*

WRITTEN EXPRESSION

There is some sense of structure to the writing, but the pupil does not use paragraphs or punctuate whole sentences accurately. Spelling is mostly secure, but 'guase' is given for 'guess'. Handwriting is legible but is not consistently well formed. However, there is a genuine attempt to present the response in Helena's own voice ('guase what'; 'I've had enough'). This piece merits a mark in the range below Level 4.

Key Considerations

- Helena's voice sustained;
- spelling generally accurate;
- limited sense of structure.

Level: below 4   *Mark: 2*

Example 12

A Midsummer Night's Dream, Act 3 Scene 2, Task 4.

What have I done to disove this. My friends are acting really strange and lest me confused. Who can I trust whos not in this Joke to.

Hermia I would have thought wouldn't carry on this game for so long, can't she see the pain shes causing me. We have been friends for years, and now shes joining forces with the two men to hurt me so.

We have never said a bad word to each other before ~~but~~ and now shes calling me names such as a Juggler and a Canker-blossom, Which made me angry and call her a counterseit and a puppet Which hurt me to say.

How long will this go on for?, and when will Lysander stop with this game to. He is In Love with Hermia and so is Demetrus so why do they both Love me now so thay say but I will have none. Hermia has already called me a thies of Love and im amazed she would think that of me.

I tried to go away back to Athens but Lysander and Demetrus both carrying

145

on with the game said they would
~~escourt~~ excort me back. Which made
Hermia even more mad and she came
for me as if I was the red sheet and
she was the bull but Lysander and
Demetrius would not let her come to
me.

I can't believe they wanted to
fight for me. Me the tall painted
maypole (as Hermia called me) who has
evermore longed to look like Hermia, is
being thought over how ridiculous!

Demetrius is the one I love and he
knows this and I know he can't stand
me, so they must think im dumb to
think that I would believe ~~them~~ that
hed love me over night. What do they
take me for! Even though I wish he
~~would~~ would love me like I love him.

I would like to know when this
will come to an end as I love them
all so very much but I don't know if
Id be able to forgive them for this
absursed behavior. I will just have to
wait and see!

Example 12

UNDERSTANDING AND RESPONSE

The pupil has presented Helena's perspective on events quite effectively in places and used quotation with genuine success, referring not only to comments made about her by Hermia, but also echoing some of her own remarks and reflecting on them (' ... and call her a counterfeit and a puppet which hurt me to say') in such a way as to imply some awareness of their effect. Helena tries here to understand why Demetrius and Lysander are behaving as they are. However, the best qualities of analysis and reflection shown in this response are not quite maintained, and comments become increasingly generalised, resulting in the piece being best described by the Level 5 performance criteria.

Key Considerations

- perceptive recreation of Helena's perspective, but not developed;
- good use of reference, but not used to explore the text further;
- some implicit awareness of the effect of language.

Level: 5+   *Mark: 12*

WRITTEN EXPRESSION

Ideas are clearly expressed and paragraphs indicate the sequence of the response, but some sentences lack coherence. Punctuation is sufficiently accurate not to impede understanding, although question marks are often missing and apostrophes are not always used. Spelling and use of capital letters is usually secure despite some lapses towards the end of the piece. An appropriate voice for Helena is generally achieved. The piece is placed in the middle of the Level 5 range.

Key Considerations

- sense clearly conveyed, but spelling and punctuation not always accurate;
- Helena's voice established.

Level: 5   *Mark: 8*

Example 13

A Midsummer Night's Dream, Act 3 Scene 2, Task 4.

I can, not belive it!
I'm so confused!, How could
they do this to me? Don't
they know it's not fair or nice
to play such a horrible joke
on me?
They know I love Demetrius and
Rr now they are using (hw) me by
saying loves me back,
It hurts that mey friends have
played such an awful game
with me.
Why is hysander and Demetrius
acting this way it's so unkind
My closest friend Hermia is even
in with the joke, how could she
do such a thing? Her of all people,
I can trust no-one as they all
seem to be in with the joke.
why has her behaviour change
so much towards me?
The things she said to me are
so cruel like " juggler, canker-blossom
thief of love.'
She has never said such
terrible things to me before

They all know I not as pretty
as Hermia, and that I cant be
loved, I'm vaunrable, yet they still
decided to ~~prock~~ scorn me.
Why is Lysander being so rude
to Hermia? calling her an
'Ethiop, cat, vile thing and serpent'
How could Hermia accuse me
of ~~stilling~~ stealing Lysander
when she knows very well that
it is Demetrius I love.
Some of the things Lysander
said to me 'stay gentle Helena.
hear my excuse, My love, my like,
my soul, fair Helena' was so
over the top. and dramtic
I thought it was terrible when
Lysander started telling me
he loved me, but Demetrius
came and joined into.
I was relived to see Hermia
Come I thought she would take Lysander
off and leave me in peace, but
no she had't to join in making
me to.
Hermia and I grew up together
~~with~~ we were like twin sisters

so close to each other.
The ' like to artificial gods,
but our 'school days, friendship,
childhood innocence?"

I feel so alone and affraid, and
very hurt that the people I once
classed as friends played such
an awful joke on me.
How could Hermia think that
I hade stolen lysander from
her, and turned him against
her.
Hermia seamed so upset and
stunned by what lysander said
to her. 'should I hurt her,
strike her dead? Although I hate,
I'll not harm her so.'
I could no longer stay there and
listen to all that scoming.
If hadn't run away Hermia would
probably of tried to harm.
For what am I to do know? where
should I go?
My friendship with Hermia could
never be the same, she has
changed so much, it's like I don't
know her anymore, she's not

the Hermia I once new.
I will never be able to trust
her again.
The language they all used
towards each other was
awful I've never ~~seen anything~~
~~like it~~ seen or heard anything
quite like.
It was a really upsetting moment
which I probably will never
forget, it will stay with me
for the rest of my life.
I still can't belive they
could treat me this way
It has really shaken me up
and turned my world upside
down.
I will never be able to forgive
them for what they put me
throughnever!

Example 13

UNDERSTANDING AND RESPONSE

This pupil sustains the role of Helena throughout, clearly conveying many different feelings. There is evidence of a firm grasp of the character, especially of her vulnerability: 'They all know I not as pretty as Hermia ...', supported by detailed reference to the text. Quotation is integrated successfully to convey the character, and shows some awareness of the effect of language, although this is not always well explained (for example, in the reference to Lysander's language being 'over the top'). The qualities of this piece therefore place it in the middle of the Level 6 range.

Key Considerations

- detailed response in parts;
- role sustained throughout;
- some awareness of language.

Level: 6   Mark: 15

WRITTEN EXPRESSION

The writing is clear and appropriately organised into paragraphs and the voice of Helena is well sustained. The choice of vocabulary is appropriate but there is a significant number of spelling mistakes, for example, 'dramtic', 'relived', and 'moking'. In places, the expression is vague: 'I thought it was terrible'; 'the language they all used towards each other was awful'. Punctuation is mostly accurate, but there are occasional grammatical errors: 'Hermia would probably of tried to harm'. The pupil keeps the reader's interest throughout, however, and therefore achieves a mark in the Level 5 band.

Key Considerations

- clearly expressed;
- voice generally well sustained;
- weak spelling.

Level: 5   Mark: 8

Example 14

A Midsummer Night's Dream, Act 3 Scene 2, Task 4.

I am totally confused! I can trust no-one, I hate men, why must they mock me, loveless Helena. Lysander has been toying with me for a few days now, showering me with false compliments and vows of love. When just last week he was going to run away with Hermia who I know is his only true love...."I had no judgment when to her I swore" Lysander said, how can I believe that? It is no coinsidence that Demetrius as well woke up and started speaking sweet romantic verse like: "O Helen, Goddes, nymph, perfect divine". It is obviously thier foul attempt at humor seeing me go from no love to both loves. Well they wont fool me, I know whats going on, I told them "Can you not hate me as I know you do?" But still they persist with a strong rivalry to mock me, when they used to be rivals for Hermia's love, so they started at eachother "You are unkind, Demetrius be not so", said Lysander then Demetrius said to Lysander "Keep thy Hermia". I cant believe any-one now. I just don't understand what would make them plot to do this to me, never have I crossed any of them. Specially Hermia.

Hermia and I have been life long friends & never have had an arguement like todays. She tries to be convincing, "What love could press Lysander from my side". But she cant trick me I know she is the main plotter of the group, so I tried to reason with her, she surly would see how much this is hurting me; "Have you not set Lysander as in scorn", to which Hermia replied: "I understand not what you mean by this". She is covering up Hermia as wicked as she is now is trying to draw the joke out for longer she pretends to be sad about why Lysander and Demetrius have stopped loving her "By why unkindly didst thou leave me so⁴?" Then I really got cross me and Hermia nearly started a physical fight. The terrible name calling she did she called me "The thief of love". Then everything I said she twisted so it sounded like I was having a go at her height "How low am I, thou painted maypoles?" Then it got physical she said "My nails can reach unto thine eyes". It took Lysander and Demetrius to get her off of me. Lysander and Demetrius began to protect me and shout terrible names at Hermia "Get you gone you dwarf"! Lysander said to her.

I can't work out why ~~the characters~~ my good friends started to behave in this manner but I do know that I stood very firm and on the outside looked like I never believed a word any of them said but inside I wish Demetrius could be true in what he says because I did love him once, and given the real chance would do it again.

It is impossible to work out where Hermia and I will go from here, I suppose it's my decision to weather I forgive her or not I just dont know why, she really went for me "And though she be but little she be fierce it got extremly convinsing. I Ijust

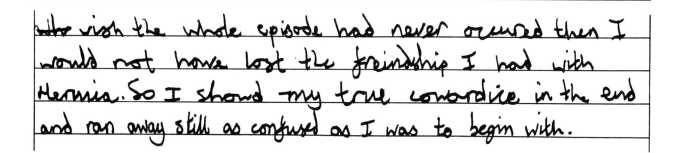

I wish the whole episode had never occured then I would not have lost the friendship I had with Hermia. So I showed my true cowardice in the end and ran away still as confused as I was to begin with.

Example 14

UNDERSTANDING AND RESPONSE

This full answer is focused and detailed, dealing with all aspects of the scene from Helena's perspective. The pupil maintains the role of Helena convincingly, showing insight into the strength and complexity of her feelings about the way she is treated by the other characters. There is also understanding of the way language contributes to and reflects the confusion in her mind, with the pupil using both explicit and implicit reference ('... she called me "The thief of love". Then everything I said she twisted ...') to what the characters say. This piece is awarded a mark in the Level 7 range as, it is clearly best described by the Level 7 performance criteria.

Key Considerations

- full, focused answer;
- understanding of language;
- appropriate references.

Level: 7   *Mark: 19*

WRITTEN EXPRESSION

This piece of writing is clearly organised and appropriate in its tone. The voice of Helena is managed consistently throughout. Paragraphing is accurate but sometimes punctuation lapses create an inappropriate confusion in over-long sentences. Spelling is usually accurate although there are errors in 'thier', 'humor', 'descision' and 'extremly'. The style is confident but not entirely successfully controlled and so a mark at the top of Level 6 is awarded.

Key Considerations

- appropriate style and tone;
- varied and appropriate vocabulary;
- lapses in punctuation and spelling.

Level: 6+   *Mark: 12*

> **Reward fully answers which provide either explicitly or implicitly an explanation of Helena's reactions to her situation and the strength of her feelings.**
>
> **Keep looking for evidence of positive achievement and if you think an answer clearly deserves a particular level, place it securely into that level.**

Content

Pupils may refer to some of the following points in their answers. These points do not imply that there is a required content. Pupils may include and develop some of these points, but not necessarily all of them or in this order.

- Helena is embarrassed by Lysander's protestations of love.

- She fears that Demetrius has joined forces with Lysander to scorn her.

- She is surprised at the way her friend Hermia, who has apparently joined 'the plot', now speaks to her.

- Helena seeks sympathy/pity from Hermia by recalling memories. She tries to get away from what she sees as the others' mockery.

- She is frightened when Lysander offers to fight Demetrius and Hermia threatens her.

- She runs away, leaving Lysander and Demetrius to fight.

Reminder

- **Pupils may make other equally creditable points.**

- **Use the performance criteria opposite in conjunction with the exemplar answers to assess the qualities of an answer on a 'best-fit' basis. Weaknesses in one area can be compensated for by strengths in another.**

- **Please refer to page 8 of the Paper 1 mark scheme for guidance on marking the work of pupils who have used an amanuensis or a mechanical aid such as a word processor.**

Fold out this flap for the performance criteria for Task 4.

A Midsummer Night's Dream Act 3 Scene 2 Task 4	
Marks available **U/R 22** **W/E 16**	In this scene Helena's world is turned upside-down. **Imagine you are Helena. Write down your thoughts and the confusion you feel as you run away.** You could begin: *I am totally confused! I can trust no one ...* Before you begin to write you should think about Helena's views on: • the strange way Lysander and Demetrius have been behaving; • Hermia's unexpected behaviour and the terrible names Hermia has called her; • the reasons the characters have been speaking and behaving in this way; • how her friendship with Hermia has changed.

Performance Criteria for UNDERSTANDING AND RESPONSE	Level	Mark
Pupils retell a few events in this scene, mainly from Helena's point of view. They include sections of the scene without any comment, offering simple opinions about the main events. Pupils may slip out of role and write about Helena in the third person.	- below 4 +	2 3 4
Pupils adopt the role of Helena but may struggle to maintain it throughout the whole of their answer. They make a few comments about her feelings or views on the other characters' behaviour with a little explanation. They retell or paraphrase some relevant parts of the scene and make references to the text without always linking them to their comments.	- 4 +	6 7 8
Pupils give an answer that provides a simple commentary, mostly from Helena's point of view. They offer an overview of Helena's character and her thoughts and feelings at this time, although their ideas may be undeveloped. Their points are illustrated by references to the text or some words or phrases used by one or more of the characters.	- 5 +	10 11 12
Pupils give a reasonably focused answer which shows some understanding of Helena's character, her confusion and the strength of her feelings. They successfully maintain the role of Helena and there is detailed reference to parts of the scene, exploring her feelings about Lysander, Demetrius and Hermia. Pupils show some awareness of the effects of the way the characters speak to each other in the scene.	- 6 +	14 15 16
Pupils give a reasonably full answer, focusing on Helena's confusion and maintaining the role of Helena convincingly. They give a detailed commentary on the scene which is closely linked to the text and shows an insight into Helena's situation and the mixed nature of her feelings. Pupils show understanding of the way the use of language contributes to the confusion and tension in the scene, selecting appropriate references to justify their ideas.	- 7 +	18 19 20
Pupils sustain the role of Helena convincingly in a confident answer which shows insight into her character and the complexities and subtleties of her situation. Well-selected references are used to develop their answers and to show appreciation of the impact of language in revealing character and attitude.	above 7	21 22

Be generous in the interpretation of what constitutes an appropriate style and form for this empathetic task. Remember that aspects of the character's role, opinions, etc. are assessed within the criteria for Understanding and Response. The focus in Written Expression should be on how well the pupils maintain their chosen style.

Pupils may, for example, adopt a colloquial style or choose to structure their answers to reflect a stream of consciousness response to the task, both of which are acceptable.

Performance Criteria for WRITTEN EXPRESSION	Level	Mark
Some of the pupils' ideas are clearly expressed. There is a limited attempt to use the chosen voice for the character. The basic grammatical structure of some sentences is correct and some punctuation is used accurately. The spelling of simple words is usually accurate and the handwriting is mostly legible though there may be obvious weaknesses in the formation of some letters.	-	1
	below 4	2
	+	3
Pupils' ideas are generally clear with some appropriate organisation. Sentence structures and vocabulary are beginning to be used to develop a voice for the character but this may not be consistently achieved. Punctuation to mark sentences is mostly used accurately and pupils are beginning to use punctuation within the sentence. The spelling of simple and common polysyllabic words is generally accurate. Handwriting is mostly clear and legible.	-	4
	4	5
	+	6
Pupils' writing is clearly expressed and usually organised into a straightforward structure or paragraphs. Vocabulary and sentence structures are sometimes chosen effectively to create an appropriate voice for the character but may not be maintained convincingly throughout. A range of punctuation, including commas, apostrophes and quotation marks, is usually used accurately. Spelling, including that of words with complex regular patterns, is usually accurate. Handwriting is generally clear and legible in a fluent style.	-	7
	5	8
	+	9
Pupils' writing is clear, structured and mostly in an appropriate style and tone for their character. The use of vocabulary and grammatical structures contribute to an appropriate tone for the voice though the same quality may not be evident throughout. A range of punctuation and paragraphing is usually used correctly to clarify meaning. Spelling is accurate though there may be some errors in difficult words. Handwriting is in a fluent and legible style.	-	10
	6	11
	+	12
Pupils' writing is confident, organised and written in an appropriate style for the character, although it may be unconvincing in tone at times. The grammatical features and choice of vocabulary are appropriate for the character and contribute to the effect of the piece. Paragraphing and punctuation are used correctly to make the sequence of thoughts and feelings clear. Spelling, including that of complex irregular words, is correct. Handwriting is in a fluent and legible style.	-	13
	7	14
	+	15
Pupils' writing is coherent and written with distinctive structural or stylistic effects appropriate to the chosen voice for the character. The precise use of vocabulary and grammatical structures enables clarity and emphasis to be achieved. Pupils show a consistent grasp of the correct use of paragraphing and a range of punctuation. Spelling, including that of complex irregular words, is correct. Handwriting is in a fluent and legible style.	above 7	16

Example 15

Romeo and Juliet, Act 2 Scenes 4-5, Task 5.

1 The nurses charicter does add humor
to these two scenes because the story
would not be right without her for
example the nurse gets involved with
the secret marrage so she will do
a lot for Julliet. When the nurse
keeps the secret safe, if it slips out
to Julliets parents then the nurse will
get fired but all she wants is for
Julliet to be happy all her life. The
nurse also gets along with Julliets
mother father and her cousen Tybalt
So she does like working as a
nurse for the capulets.
2 She also gets on with Romeo
and Mercutio two friends from the
arch enemys the montagues. Romeo
montague is who Julliet is secretly
getting married to!!! Mercutio is a
young friend of Romeo's and likes
the nurse but teases her by calling
her an ancient lady then sings
that passage a few more times. But
the nurse has come to ignore Mercutio
by calling him a saucy merchant

that was so full of himself. Romeo explains he is just been imature and trying to be funny.

The nurse sees that and says "And 'a speak anything against me, I'll take him down and 'a luster that he is and twenty such jacks and if canot I will find those who can, I am none of his flirt-gills."

3. Mercutio gets along with the nurse but is too cheeky for his own good Romeo on the other hand is not cheeky like mercutio and speaks to the nurse like any civilised adult should. Julliet treats the nurse well and asks her why she looks so sad the nurse answers that she is weary, give her leave a while and how her bones ache. Then all of a sudden the nurse must feel better because she asks Julliet is she sure of the choice of man she has made. Julliet answers. Yes yes I have made my definate choice. Then the nurse for some reason comes on with a headache. Julliet asked where her mother is the nurse answers

Are you so hot? So the nurse is chaning to subject from Julliets Mother to something else.

4. The nurse acts like she is Julliets mother and has been the family nurse for a long long time she even looked after Julliets mother and father. She is alway checking up on Julliet to see if she is aliright. She always sees Romeo about the marrage.

Example 15

UNDERSTANDING AND RESPONSE

The pupil follows the guidance of the prompts to generate some explanation and comment but is more secure writing about character than humour. There are references to the text ('calling him a saucy merchant') and direct quotation, although these are not supported by further comment. However, explanations such as 'Romeo ... is not cheeky like mercutio and speaks ... like any civilised adult should' show the pupil has recognised there are different exchanges in the scene which teach us things about the Nurse. A mark at the top end of Level 4 is appropriate.

Key Considerations

- comment and a little explanation;
- references to text;
- focus mainly on character.

Level: 4+   Mark: 8

WRITTEN EXPRESSION

The pupil makes use of the prompts to provide a straightforward structure for this response. The range of vocabulary and sentence structures used is limited, but meaning is generally clear. Accurate punctuation is used to demarcate sentences, but the spelling of polysyllabic words is erratic; 'headache' and 'involved' are correctly spelled, but 'chariter', and 'famly' are not. Handwriting is clear and legible. A mark in the middle of Level 4 is justified.

Key Considerations

- clear organisation;
- mostly accurate sentence punctuation;
- simple and common polysyllabic words not always accurately spelt.

Level: 4   Mark: 5

Example 16

Romeo and Juliet, Act 2 Scenes 4-5, Task 5.

In these two scenes, you get a better idea of the nurse's character. You find out that she is quite 'tubby', when Mercutio and friends mock her by saying, "a sail, a sail". Meaning she is like a boat, because she is 'big'.

These scenes add to the nurses humor, not particually in the first scene shown (Act 2 scene 4), but more in (Act 2 scene 5)

In each scene she has a different humor. In Scene 4 (Act 2), she seems to play along with Mercutios mockery, which is quite a contrast to her own. Mercutio is a born joker, where as the nurse, can be serious some times.

In scene 5 (Act 2), she seems more humoraus, as she keeps juliet in suspense. She complains that her bones ache, and "Do you not see that I am out of breath". Juliet then replies that she must have breath, to say she is out of breath. In this scene it is quite funny to see how juliet is eager to know of the news, but the nurse keeps delaying it.

Juliet, in (Act 2 scene 5) is also quite funny, but she doesn't know it, for example when she was talking about the 'death' incident.

The nurse's humor in these two scenes is quite a contrast. The humor in the first scene seems to be more like 'funny comments', where as in the second scene her humor is more 'practical'. When i say 'practical', I don't mean 'practical joke', but her actions are funny.

The different ways in which the nurse speaks to Romeo and Mercutio, are also quite funny. To Mercutio the comments she makes seem to 'challenge' Mercutio to say something funny each time. When she speaks to Romeo, however, her jokes aren't really jokes, they are just funny things underlined in the text. For example when she curses Mercutio for being a 'saucy merchant'. She also compares many things to each other. ie. Romeo to Rosmary.

The characters the nurse has contact with, all seem to have some humor.

Mercutio, as I have mentioned earlier, as the boom joker, seems to succeed in all the challenges that the nurse gives to him. (Well that is the way I see it!) i.e. challenge- Is it good den? Answer by Mercutio- 'Tis no less, I tell ye, for the bawdy hand of the dial is now upon the prick of noon'. You can imagine these two characters saying this, and Mercutio's friends laughing along with him.

Romeo treats the nurse in a different way. He first mocks her when she asks Romeo if he knows where to find Romeo. He then asks many questions, but seems more serious then. It is still quite funny, though, to look at some of the comments they make.

Juliets scene is the funniest though, (according to me!), as I have mentioned earlier, it is funny to see her eagerness. The tension is built up as the nurse keeps delaying the news of the marriage to juliet. Finally at the end of the scene she tells juliet of the marriage.

The nurse, acting as a messenger between Romeo and Juliet. I think she agrees with the marriage, but would prefer it to be kept a secret. I think secretly she would prefer Juliet to marry Paris. I also think she doesn't really know what to feel, as if she agrees to the marriage, then when Lady Capulet or Capulet found out, they would be angered because she was made for her suitor not her enemy.

All of these points covered in my essay, show the nurses character. It proves that she is funny, faithful (to Juliet), and always wants the best for her lady (Juliet). She also likes to hold people in suspence. I see the nurse generally as a funny nice person to be with.

Example 16

UNDERSTANDING AND RESPONSE

This response works its way through the scene offering a quite focused account of the way humour is created by the Nurse's words and actions. Appropriate references are given, and there is an attempt to define the effect of her exchanges with Mercutio – 'she seems to play along with Mercutios mockery'. This is contrasted with the way she uses 'suspense' to create humour with Juliet and what the pupil calls 'practical' humour, in other words the way she acts. This is a methodical attempt to explore parts of the text, with an overall view of the Nurse's character and the different ways humour is generated. Hence, a mark in Level 6 is the best fit.

Key Considerations

- reasonably focused with some detail;
- understanding of Nurse's character;
- comments on how humour is created in the exchanges between the characters.

Level: 6   *Mark: 15*

WRITTEN EXPRESSION

The writing is clear and well organised into paragraphs. An appropriate rather than a wide range of vocabulary is used so that meaning is immediately clear, although sometimes this pupil has to work hard to achieve clarity, for example, the explanation of how, in the second scene, the Nurse's humour is 'more practical'. There is some variety of sentence structure, but again there are occasions where control is not secure and commas are used to link sentences which should have been more tightly organised. There are few errors in spelling and a range of punctuation is employed but not always accurately. Handwriting is fluent and legible. The overall confidence of the writing, despite some unevenness, justifies a Level 6 mark.

Key Considerations

- well organised and paragraphed with meaning clear;
- occasional lack of control in sentence structuring;
- few technical weaknesses.

Level: 6   *Mark: 11*

Example 17

Romeo and Juliet, Act 2 Scenes 4-5, Task 5.

In these two scenes you learn that the nurse is very pleased to be involved with the secret marriage plans. She is also involved because she wants to make Juliet 'happy'. When she says "Lord, Lord she will be a joyful woman" it is obvious that she is happy too because she knows that Juliet will be thrilled by the news.

When the nurse first goes to get Romeo she encounters Mercutio, and he and Romeo begin to torment her. Mercutio becomes very crude and starts making sexual puns. Even though the nurse seems to find these funny she insists on keeping a straight face and acting 'lady like' Mercutio then continues and when the Nurse says to Romeo:

'I desire some confidence with you' Mercutio and Benvolio immediately think she is a prostitute.

After Mercutio and Benvolio leave the Nurse is quite upset but even more angry. She refers to Mercutio as a 'saucy merchant' and a 'saucy knave'. The funny bit is when she turns on Peter and begins to curse him for not standing by her she says that 'He must suffer every knave to use her at his pleasure" Peter argues that he 'saw no man use her at

167

his pleasure'. This angers the Nurse greatly but after the satisfaction of naming Mercutio a 'Scurvy Knave' again she then gets back to the matter in hand and acts as if nothing has happened.

When the Nurse and Romeo have finished making the arrangements she gets back to her old self and begins ranting and Raving about Juliet and how Paris also wants her hand in Marriage. ~~stop~~

"Well sir, my ~~misshess~~ mistress is the sweetest lady - Lord, Lord! When 'twas a prating thing -" This is where she begins talking of Juliet and then she remembers about Paris and tells Romeo;

"-There is a nobleman in town, one Paris, that would ~~~~ fain lay a knife aboard;" She tells this to Romeo to make him worry and to let him know that Juliet is in demand. Straight after though she tells him that Juliet see's Paris as a 'Toad' and that he should not worry.

The Nurse also makes a joke about how Romeo's name begins with 'R' and how that is the 'dog-name'.

Juliet is very annoyed that the Nurse has taken so long to ~~~~ return and when she does, Juliet tries 'buttering her-up' to get the ~~information~~ information she needs quickly without the nurse getting started. She asks the Nurse to ~~~~ send

Peter away and then she says:

"Good sweet Nurse — O Lord, why look'st thou
sad?"

Here the nurse has deliberately put on a sad
face just to get Juliet worried and it works.

The Nurse then tries to put off telling
Juliet the news by saying:

"I am a-weary, give me leave a while.
Fie, how my bones ache! What a jaunce have
I!"

~~She te'~~ In ~~this~~ these lines she tells Juliet that she
is tired and wants to be left alone. She
also says that she has had a bumpy,
exaughsting journey. Juliet persists and the
Nurse complains that "She is out of Breath"
Juliet replies with:

"How art thou ~~out~~ of breath, when thou hast breath,
To ~~tell~~ Say to me thou art out of breath?" This
is a very clever answer and it gets the nurse
talking about Romeo. She begins nattering as
usual and starts to contradict herself saying
at first that Juliet has 'made a simple choice' and
then that Romeo is 'as gentle as a lamb'.

When Juliet starts getting inpatient again
and whinning the Nurse goes back to ~~complaining~~
complaining about her aches and pains. She
then begins enquiring about where Lady Capulet

is and this frustrates Juliet ~~ever~~ even more.
The nurse then says:
"Is this the poultice for my aching bones?
Henceforward do your messages yourself." This
shows that the nurse is fed up of taking
messages for Juliet if this is the thanks she
gets.
The Nurse then gets soft again and begins
to tell Juliet the plan. It is obvious that
the Nurse is ~~to~~ just as excited about the
arrangement as Juliet is.
I think that the Nurse is one of
the funniest characters in the play and
if she weren't in this scene it would be
dull and boring. She really brightens up
the whole play.

Example 17

UNDERSTANDING AND RESPONSE

This response works its way through the scene offering a detailed and quite focused commentary. The pupil understands how the Nurse's character and behaviour add to the humour of the scene. Appropriate references are given and there is some awareness of how language creates humour, for example the ambiguity in the use of the word 'pleasure': 'The funny bit is when she turns on Peter'. This pupil offers an exploration of the text line by line rather than a more general discussion of the ways aspects of the Nurse's character contribute to humour, but nevertheless is described by enough of the criteria in the Level 7 band to be placed just into it.

Key Considerations

- reasonably focused and detailed;
- understanding of the Nurse's character;
- comments on how language contributes to humour.

Level: 7-   Mark: 18

WRITTEN EXPRESSION

This writing is confident, well organised and in a usually appropriate style although it occasionally lapses into a slightly less suitable style, using phrases such as 'ranting and Raving', '"buttering her-up"' and 'The Nurse then gets soft'. The vocabulary is varied and usually communicates meaning precisely ('she encounters Mercutio'; 'to torment her'; 'after the saticfaction of naming Mercutio') while paragraphing and punctuation are correctly used. Spelling is mostly correct and handwriting is in a fluent and legible style. A mark in the middle of Level 7 is justified.

Key Considerations

- confident and organised;
- effective vocabulary;
- correct spelling.

Level: 7   Mark: 14

> Some pupils will base their answers on a study of the text of this scene while others may focus in detail on a performance. The performance criteria can apply to both these approaches and both should be given equal credit.
>
> Keep looking for evidence of positive achievement and if you think an answer clearly deserves a particular level, place it securely into that level.

Content

Pupils may refer to some of the following points in their answers. These points do not imply that there is a required content. Pupils may include and develop some of these points, but not necessarily all of them or in this order.

- The Nurse enjoys her role as go-between. She shows her affection for Juliet and her faithfulness as a servant.

- With Mercutio, the Nurse offers and receives bawdy humour. She attempts to speak to Romeo with more respect, wishing to impress him and seeking assurance that Romeo will treat Juliet honourably. Humour is created by the Nurse's attempts to be formal.

- Mercutio is disrespectful to the Nurse who is treated as a figure of fun. However, Romeo and Juliet trust the Nurse and rely on her as a go-between.

- The Nurse builds up Juliet's feeling of suspense by taking her time about passing on Romeo's message.

Reminder

- **Pupils may make other equally creditable points.**

- **Use the performance criteria opposite in conjunction with the exemplar answers to assess the qualities of an answer on a 'best-fit' basis. Weaknesses in one area can be compensated for by strengths in another.**

- **Please refer to page 8 of the Paper 1 mark scheme for guidance on marking the work of pupils who have used an amanuensis or a mechanical aid such as a word processor.**

Fold out this flap for the performance criteria for Task 5.

Romeo and Juliet Act 2 Scenes 4-5 Task 5			
Marks available **U/R 22** **W/E 16**	In these scenes the Nurse is the messenger between Romeo and Juliet. **What do you learn about the Nurse and how does her character add to the humour in these scenes?** Before you begin to write you should think about: • the Nurse's feelings about her involvement in the secret arrangements; • how the differences in the way the Nurse speaks to Romeo and Mercutio are amusing; • the humour in the different ways Mercutio, Romeo and Juliet treat the Nurse; • how the Nurse's behaviour towards Juliet adds humour.		

Performance Criteria for UNDERSTANDING AND RESPONSE	Level	Mark
Pupils make a few simple comments about the Nurse or about the humour in these scenes, but they may not refer to all the characters. They retell parts of the scenes and their answers are only partly relevant. They give references without explanation.	- **below 4** +	2 3 4
Pupils make some comments about the Nurse's character with a little explanation. They recognise some aspects of the humour but focus mostly on character. They retell or paraphrase some relevant parts of the scenes and make references but without always linking them to their comments.	- **4** +	6 7 8
Pupils give an answer which provides simple commentary. They offer an overview of the scenes, showing understanding of the Nurse's character and how she adds humour, though their ideas may be undeveloped. Their points are illustrated by references to the text or some words or phrases used by one or more of the characters.	- **5** +	10 11 12
Pupils give a reasonably focused answer with some exploration of the text. They offer a detailed commentary on some aspects of the scenes showing some understanding of the Nurse's character and how it adds to the humour. They make straightforward comments on the way the language of the scene is used to create humour, making use of appropriate references to support their ideas.	- **6** +	14 15 16
Pupils give a reasonably full answer which shows engagement with the text and the character of the Nurse. They give a detailed commentary on the scenes which shows insight into the different ways the Nurse is presented and how her character adds to the humour. They recognise how language contributes to the presentation of character and humour and they justify their comments by the use of carefully selected references to the text.	- **7** +	18 19 20
Pupils give a confident and sustained answer which shows an ability to evaluate the way the Nurse is presented. Well-selected references are used to illustrate and justify their comments and explain their appreciation of the contribution of language to the presentation of character and the creation of humour.	**above 7**	21 22

Performance Criteria for WRITTEN EXPRESSION	Level	Mark
Some of the pupils' ideas are clearly expressed. The basic grammatical structure of some sentences is correct and some punctuation is used accurately. The spelling of simple words is usually accurate and the handwriting is mostly legible, though there may be obvious weaknesses in the formation of some letters.	- / below 4 / +	1 / 2 / 3
Pupils' ideas are generally clear with some appropriate organisation. Sentence structures and vocabulary are beginning to be used effectively to develop a point of view. Punctuation to mark sentences is mostly used accurately and pupils are beginning to use punctuation within the sentence. The spelling of simple and common polysyllabic words is generally accurate. Handwriting is mostly clear and legible.	- / 4 / +	4 / 5 / 6
Pupils' writing is clearly expressed and usually organised into a straightforward structure or paragraphs. Vocabulary and sentence structures are sometimes chosen effectively to clarify and develop their point of view, but may not be maintained convincingly throughout. A range of punctuation, including commas, apostrophes and quotation marks, is usually used accurately. Spelling, including that of words with complex regular patterns, is usually accurate. Handwriting is generally clear and legible in a fluent style.	- / 5 / +	7 / 8 / 9
Pupils' writing is clear, structured and mostly in an appropriate style for a discursive piece. The use of vocabulary and grammatical structures, together with appropriate paragraphing, contribute to the clarity of the writing though the same quality may not be evident throughout. A range of punctuation is usually used correctly to clarify meaning. Spelling is accurate, though there may be some errors in difficult words. Handwriting is in a fluent and legible style.	- / 6 / +	10 / 11 / 12
Pupils' writing is confident and organised, and it is in an appropriate style although it may be unsophisticated in tone at times. Ideas are developed by a range of grammatical features and the effective use of vocabulary. Paragraphing and punctuation are used to make the sequence of ideas clear. Spelling, including that of complex irregular words, is correct. Handwriting is in a fluent and legible style.	- / 7 / +	13 / 14 / 15
Pupils' writing presents arguments clearly in a coherent way. The choice of style and structure, supported by the precise use of vocabulary and grammatical structures, enables clarity and emphasis to be achieved. Pupils show a consistent grasp of the correct use of paragraphing and a range of punctuation. Spelling, including that of complex irregular words, is correct. Handwriting is in a fluent and legible style.	above 7	16

Example 18

Romeo and Juliet, Act 3 Scene 1, Task 6.

Tension is created in the opening of the scene by Benvolio saying The day is hot, the capels are abroad The tension is hot, clamy and dry. Benvolio then says By my head, here come the Capulets.

Mercutio's and Tybalt's words and actions build up tension and excitement by cracking jokes about Romeo to try and get a fight. Mercutio says "Men's eyes where made to look, and let them gaze. Benvolio wants to make Mercutio retire but Mercutio wants to start the fight.

Romeo says villain am I none; So that gets Mercutio even more worked up. So the tension gets bad. worst. The arrival of the prince adds to the tension at the end of the scene beacause nothing happens to anybody and you don't know if they are going to meet the next day.

Shakespeare builds up tension and excitement in this scene by having Mercutio in a fightative mood

and by having Mercutio the play
set on a hot day. The tension
and excitement builds up by having
Mercutio as a bad fighting caracter
and by having Benvolio as his friend
and ~~as~~ having him keeping all the ~~plce~~
plece works quite well because you
never know when Benvolio is going to
turn on Mercutio for afight also
the tension builds up by it being
such a ~~fite~~ quick ~~day~~ play.
Shakespeare has made the charaters
~~to~~ have mood swings and which
makes the play exciting.

Shakespeare also gets more people
involved so that also makes in more
exciting because they all get shouting
at each other.

Example 18

UNDERSTANDING AND RESPONSE

The response focuses on some significant moments that contribute to tension in the scene, but comment is limited. Some of the references (to the weather, to the mood of the characters) are relevant, though made repetitively, but others are not: for example, 'the tension builds up by it being such a quick play'. There is a certain amount of paraphrase, with quotation not really integrated into the narrative. Comments on Mercutio ('in a fightative mood' and 'a bad fighting caracter') suggest partial understanding. The mark awarded puts the piece in the middle of Level 4.

Key Considerations

- some attempt to focus on elements of tension;
- a little comment and explanation;
- references not always linked to comments.

Level: 4   Mark: 7

WRITTEN EXPRESSION

The ideas in this response are generally expressed clearly and appropriately organised, though there is a certain amount of repetition of phrases. Punctuation of sentences is adequate but there is little evidence of punctuation within sentences. The quality of writing deteriorates towards the end. Spelling is not consistent. Handwriting is clear and legible. The piece is therefore placed at the top of the Level 4 band.

Key Considerations

- sense clearly conveyed, but spelling and punctuation not consistent;
- quality of writing not sustained.

Level: 4+   Mark: 6

Example 19

Romeo and Juliet, Act 3 Scene 1, Task 6.

Shakespeare builds up tension at the start of the ~~play~~ scene because Mercutio and Benvolio start quarelling over silly, little things. Mercutio is saying that Benvolio argues over nothing worth arguing about e.g Mercutio says that Benvolio would argue with some-one who ties his new shoes with old riband.

After this Tybalt, Petruchio and the others enter in the market place. The two families spot each other and Tybalt walks up to them (Benvolio & Mercutio) Tybalt is being friendly and asks one of them for a word. Mercutio is feeling a little angry now and treats Tybalt like he has done some-thing wrong.

Mercutio and Tybalt then build up tension and excitement as they start arguing more, each sentence getting more voilent.

The argument gradually brings in swords to which Benvolio says "Either withdraw into some private place or reason coldly of your grievances (etc)."

Now the audience knows that there is going to be some trouble.

After this Romeo enters which causes more bother towards the arguement in the market place. When Romeo enters he walks up to Tybalt, Mercutio etc.

→ Romeo says in a calm way to Tybalt that he doesn't want to fight.

Romeo says this because he is getting married to Juliet and he doesn't want no trouble between Juliet and him-self. Tybalt takes no notice of Romeo and so Tybalt draws his sword Romeo tells him that he loves him but Tybalt ignores him and they both start fighting.

Whilst Tybalt and Mercutio are fighting Romeo tries to

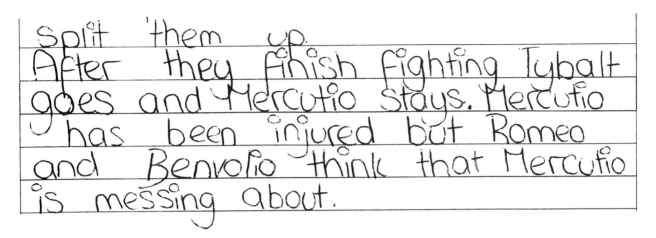

split 'them up.
After they finish fighting Tybalt
goes and Mercutio stays. Mercutio
has been injured but Romeo
and Benvolio think that Mercutio
is messing about.

Example 19

UNDERSTANDING AND RESPONSE

The pupil's approach is mainly narrative, but shows understanding of the significant features by highlighting the stages of development in the quarrel between Mercutio and Tybalt. Only one quotation is used, with an appropriate but limited comment to follow: 'Now the audience knows that there is going to be some trouble'. There is some discussion of Romeo's motivation but it is only partially focused on the text: 'he is getting married to Juliet and he doesn't want no trouble between Juliet and him-self'. The response disregards a significant section of the scene but nevertheless does provide an overview of some of the ways tension and excitement are generated. There is some implicit awareness of language ('they start arguing more, each sentence getting more voilent'; 'Romeo says in a calm way') but little explicit reference to the text at all. On the 'best-fit' basis, a mark in the Level 5 range is justified.

Key Considerations

- some understanding of significant features giving overview of the scene;
- little use of appropriate quotation.

Level: 5   Mark: 11

WRITTEN EXPRESSION

The ideas in this response are reasonably clearly expressed, using simple vocabulary and basic organisation. Punctuation is mainly limited to full stops. Spelling is generally sound. Handwriting is legible throughout. The pupil's written expression is best described by the Level 5 performance criteria.

Key Considerations

- straightforward presentation and expression;
- punctuation basic but adequate; spelling usually accurate.

Level: 5-   Mark: 7

Example 20

Romeo and Juliet, Act 3 Scene 1, Task 6.

In the opening scenes of Act 3 the tension is created by the fact that it is hot and everybody is moody and bored. ~~The~~ Benvolio and Mercutio are sitting talking when Tybalt and men arrive from the other family. This causes tension because Tybalt is looking for Romeo and he is very angry.

Romeo is a Montague and he was at the Capulets party and Tybalt didn't like it so thats why Tybalt is angry and looking for Romeo.

~~Tybalt~~ Tybalt starts to talk to Benvolio and Mercutio and starts to get a bit uptight. They are just about to start to argue when Romeo arrives. When he arrives he builds up tension just by arriving but then it is still created by Tybalt using the words 'thou art a villain' to speak about Romeo. Romeo is not happy and says in return 'Villain am I none; Therefore farewell, I see tho knowest me not'.

Tybalt says to Romeo to draw out his sword but mercutio jumps into the way as says calm down, then draws out his own sword. Tybalt draws his out too and they fight.

This causes ~~a lot~~ alot of tension and

and excitement in the audience and in the scenes.

Romeo straight away says to stop the fight because it is forbiden in Verona streets.

This causes some more tension because Romeo is trying to break the fight up but they are still trying to fight.

Romeo stops the fight and as doing so Tybalt, under Romeos arm thrusts mercutio.

The tension is increased in the scene but it calms down a bit because the characters are all shocked including the victim Tybalt. At this stage the tension is quite large. Tybalt leaves the scene and his men follow.

Mercutio insists that someone goes and fetches a surgeon. Romeo doesn't realise how bad the wound is. Mercutio starts to say that Romeo shouldn't have come between them because he got stabbed under Romeo's arm. The tension is easing off a bit because they are worried about mercutio but they are still very angry with Tybalt and his men.

Mercutio leaves with Benvolio and leaves Romeo alone. to calm down.

Benvolio enters the scene again and pronounces that Mercutio has died.

Tybalt enters again and the tension increases again.

Romeo and Tybalt start to quarell and Romeo says 'take back 'villain' again', he then later in his ~~speec~~ speech says 'Either thou or I, or both, must go with him.'

They fight and the tension is still high because of Mercutios death and Tybalts anger with Romeo.

Tybalt falls to the ground.

~~The~~ ~~ea~~ Benvolio says to Romeo he must leave.

The citizens and officers arrive - They ask Benvolio where the murderer of Tybalt has run ~~~~ to.

The tension is still high because Romeo has hurt Tybalt and he is on the floor but no-one apart from Benvolio, Tybalt and Romeo knows what happened to Tybalt.

The prince arrives and Montague, Capulet, their wives and all the family.

The tension is very big now and it built up all the way through from the begining of the scene where Tybalt was looking for Romeo.

Benvolio tells the prince whats happened between Tybalt and mercutio and Tybalt and Romeo. The prince decides to banishe Romeo.

The tension through that scene was very big most of the way through. I think it is good the way Shakespeare has built it up gradually leading to the banishment of Romeo.

I think the words, actions and behaviour of all the characters was strong and that all added to the tension.

At the end the tension is very big because Romeo has been banished, Tybalt and mercutio has been killed.

Example 20

UNDERSTANDING AND RESPONSE

This pupil attempts to focus on the tension and excitement in the scene but does so by describing the main events and commenting on particularly tense moments. There is an initial focus on the mood and atmosphere at the beginning of the scene and, in the context of the play, the arrival at that point of Tybalt 'causes tension'. The increasingly angry exchanges with Mercutio and the entry of Romeo are mentioned although there are some misjudgements ('mercutio jumps into the way as says calm down' and 'The tension is easing off a bit because they are worried about Mercutio'). The account continues with reference to the fight between Tybalt and Romeo and concludes with the arrival of the Prince and an attempt to offer an overview of the tension throughout the scene. In summary, this pupil has provided a simple commentary on the scene with sufficient focus on the task and the way tension is created to justify a mark at the bottom of the Level 6 range, despite some misunderstanding and the virtual absence of any comment on 'excitement'.

Key Considerations

- simple commentary on the scene;
- straightforward focus on the ways tension is created;
- points not explored and some misunderstanding.

Level: 6-   Mark: 14

WRITTEN EXPRESSION

This pupil's response is generally expressed clearly and is reasonably well organised with some attempt to use paragraphs. There is some variety of sentence structures, but vocabulary is not always appropriate ('tension is easing off a bit' and 'The tension is very big now'). Sentences are generally demarcated accurately, but little other use is made of punctuation. There are few spelling errors and handwriting is in a fluent and legible style. On the 'best-fit' principle, a mark at the top of the Level 5 range is justified.

Key Considerations

- clearly organised and expressed;
- some variety of sentence structures but vocabulary not always appropriately used;
- limited range of punctuation.

Level: 5+   Mark: 9

Example 21

Romeo and Juliet, Act 3 Scene 1, Task 6.

Act 3 Scene 1, provides a major turning point to the story. This scene is a very eventfull scene, in which two main characters who form the plot the excitment in the plot, are slain. Mercutio, a good friend of Romeo's is stabbed by Tybalt, cousin to Romeo's newly wed Juliet. The events leading up to the actual fight are very well written as they build up an air of suspense and uncertainty.

At the opening of the scene, Benvolio and Mercutio (two of Romeo's closest friends) are strolling through Verona Square. The sun is beating down on them and Mercutio is in high spirits. Benvolio knows that the Capulet boys are around somewhere and trys to persuade Mercutio to calm down and leave the area. He does this as he knows that if they should meet the Capulets, they will not be able to avoid a confrontation. "I pray thee, good Mercutio, let's retire: the day is hot, the Capels are abroad, and if we meet we shall not scape abroad".

At hearing this, Mercutio becomes even more high spirited. He starts to accuse Benvolio of being the only trouble maker (which is quite untrue) and makes up great speeches about Benvolio's hot temper. "Thou wilt quarrel with a man that hath a hair more or a hair less in his beard than thou hast..." During the time that this is happening, the reader can tell that something is going to happen involving Benvolio, Mercutio and the Capulet Boys.

Mercutio kontinues to taunt Benvolio, but with no real affect," Thou hast quarelled with a man for coughing in the street, because he hath wakened thy dog that hath lain asleep in the sun..."

Thou the Cap At line 30, the Capulets arrive. This sentence from Benvolio and Mercutio, "By my head, here come the Capulets" "By my heel, I care not." adds greatly to the excitment of the scene, as we can tell that Mercutio is up for trouble. Tybalt enters and asks to speak to one of them, "Gentlemen, good den , a word with one of you." to which Mercutio replies in a taunting manner," And but one word with one of us? Couple it with something, make it a word and a blow!"

Already, Shakespeare has built up tension by showing friction between his fiery characters. Mercutio and Tybalt continue to goad each other until Romeo enters. We know from previous scenes, that Tybalt is furious with Romeo. This is because Tybalt tried to get rid of him at Lord Capulets party, but was put in his place by the Lord and was told to let Romeo be. This infuriated Tybalt and so is out to get Romeo.

When Romeo enters, he has an immediate effect on the scene. We can sense Tybalts anger through his language," Romeo, the love I bear thee can afford no better term than this: Thou art a villain." Romeo then, unmeaningly, insults him even more by his calm

gentlemanner and the forgiving language he uses.
"Tybalt, the reason that I have to love thee doth much
excuse the appertaining rage to such a greeting..." by this
Romeo means that he excuses Tybalts ~~remarks~~ insults as he
has just married his cousin Juliet and so therefore must love
him. Tybalt becomes so infuriated by Romeos remarks
that he ~~starts to~~ loses control and challenges Romeo to a
duel, "Boy, this shall not excuse the injuries that thou
hast done me, therefore turn and draw. ✗ This section of
the scene provides a very climatic and exciting part as
the reader is left in suspense as to what Romeo will
do. ✱ The language Tybalt ~~Rom~~

✱   uses towards Romeo infuriates Mercutio so much
that he accepts Tybalts challenge to Romeo and starts
to abuse Tybalt verbally. He uses very clever language ~~with~~
which adds to the suspense as to what will happen
next, "Tybalt, you rat catcher, will you walk", "Good king
of cats..." ~~this~~ His language is clever as it provokes Tybalt
by insulting his name.

        They draw their weapons but Romeo trys to stop
them "Tybalt, Mercutio, the Prince expressly hath forbid
this bandying in Verona streets". "Hold Tybalt, Good
Mercutio!" A real shock happens at this point, as Tybalt
stabs Mercutio and then retreats. At first we do not
realise that Mercutio is fatally wounded, because he
continues to use jovial and tricky language "Ay, ay,
a scratch, a scratch, marry, tis enough..." Slowly the reader

187

then realizes the horror of the situation as Mercutio passes away. Now we are left with a very exciting situation. Shakespeare writes in this context so that we are left wondering what Romeo will do. To the readers shock, Romeo follows Tybalt and kills him, through a haze of sweat and tears for his best friends death.

Now the tension is built up unbelievably as we knew that the penalty for murder, is death! This leaves the reader wondering exactly what our hero, Romeo, will do, as he cannot die after just marrying Juliet!

Finally to our horror, the Prince turns up. Now we are sure that Romeo must die, as it was the Prince himself who issued the law, but Shakespeare manages to produce another great twist as he lets Romeo off with only banishment! Lady Capulet (who has just arrived) is furious about this decision as she hates Romeo. She leaves the scene with this, "Romeo slew Tybalt, Romeo must not live!" As she now exits we are left in great suspense as to what she will do. The Prince pardons Romeo, "Immediately we do exile him hence" and so the scene closes.

I think Shakespeare has done an excellent job of providing excitement and suspense to the scene. He used clever and interesting language along with unsuspected events, to produce what I think is "a masterful piece!"

Example 21

UNDERSTANDING AND RESPONSE

This is a confident, well-informed and detailed answer from the effective opening to the appreciation at the end of the impact of the Prince's arrival. Quotations and references are well integrated with detailed commentary and explanation. The build-up of tension and excitement via dramatic structure and language is explored and analysed in some detail. Such a sustained answer clearly indicates achievement above Level 7.

Key Considerations

- confident and sustained;
- appreciation of dramatic structure and language.

Level: above 7   Mark: 21

WRITTEN EXPRESSION

This pupil's writing is confident and controlled. There are a few spelling errors (such as 'excitment', 'writen', 'firey') and there are a few lapses in punctuation and the precise use of vocabulary ('unmeaningly', 'A real shock happens at this point'). However, the overall impression is of good paragraph control, general accuracy and an effective and mature use of vocabulary ('confrontation', 'taunt', 'by showing friction', 'infuriated'). These strengths, balanced against the errors, justify a mark above Level 7.

Key Considerations

- confident and organised;
- effective, varied vocabulary;
- correct paragraphing.

Level: above 7   Mark: 16

Some pupils will base their answers on a study of the text of this scene while others may focus in detail on a performance. The performance criteria can apply to both these approaches and both should be given equal credit.

Keep looking for evidence of positive achievement and if you think an answer clearly deserves a particular level, place it securely into that level.

Content

Pupils may refer to some of the following points in their answers. These points do not imply that there is a required content. Pupils may include and develop some of these points, but not necessarily all of them or in this order.

- It is hot, and as Benvolio points out, the Capulets are 'abroad' and 'the mad blood is stirring'.

- Mercutio is in an irritable mood and is ready to provoke and be provoked.

- Tybalt is angry with Romeo and determined to fight him.

- The verbal exchanges between Mercutio and Benvolio turn to more serious sparring between Mercutio and Tybalt.

- Romeo's attempt to achieve peace and reconciliation inflames Tybalt. The scene becomes more tense and dramatic, and can only end in tragedy.

- The Prince has the power to determine what will happen to the characters. His arrival creates a mood of anticipation.

Reminder

- **Pupils may make other equally creditable points.**

- **Use the performance criteria opposite in conjunction with the exemplar answers to assess the qualities of an answer on a 'best-fit' basis. Weaknesses in one area can be compensated for by strengths in another.**

- **Please refer to page 8 of the Paper 1 mark scheme for guidance on marking the work of pupils who have used an amanuensis or a mechanical aid such as a word processor.**

Printed in the United kingdom for The Stationery Office
J71872 C20 2/99 9385 9823

Fold out this flap for the performance criteria for Task 6.

Romeo and Juliet Act 3 Scene 1 Task 6	
Marks available **U/R 22** **W/E 16**	From the beginning of this scene the audience realises that the feud between the families will lead to tragedy. **Explain in detail how you think Shakespeare builds up tension and excitement in this scene.** Before you begin to write you should think about: • how tension is created in the opening of the scene (lines 1 - 48); • how Mercutio's and Tybalt's words and actions build up tension and excitement; • how Romeo's words and behaviour add to the tension; • how the arrival of the Prince adds to the tension at the end of the scene.

Performance Criteria for UNDERSTANDING AND RESPONSE	Level	Mark
Pupils make a few simple comments about what happens in this scene with some reference to the idea of tension or excitement. They retell parts of the scene and their answers are only partly relevant. They give references without explanation.	- below 4 +	2 3 4
Pupils make some comments about significant moments or events in this scene with a little explanation. They recognise some aspects of the scene which contribute to the tension or excitement. They retell or paraphrase some relevant parts of the scene and make references but without always linking them to their comments.	- 4 +	6 7 8
Pupils give an answer which provides a simple commentary. They offer an overview of the scene, showing understanding of some of the significant features which add to a feeling of tension and excitement. Their points are illustrated by references to the text or some words or phrases used by one or more of the characters.	- 5 +	10 11 12
Pupils give a reasonably focused answer with some exploration of the text. They offer a detailed commentary on some aspects of the scene, showing some understanding of the different ways a feeling of tension and excitement is built up. They give straightforward comments on how the way the characters speak to each other contributes to the atmosphere, making use of appropriate references to support their ideas.	- 6 +	14 15 16
Pupils give a reasonably full answer which shows engagement with the text and a grasp of the task. They give a detailed commentary on the scene, focusing on the different ways a feeling of tension and excitement is built up. They show understanding of the way Shakespeare's use of language contributes to the mood and atmosphere and they justify their comments by the use of carefully selected references to the text.	- 7 +	18 19 20
Pupils give a confident and sustained answer which shows an appreciation of the different ways tension and excitement are built up through dramatic structure and language. Well-selected references are used to illustrate and justify their comments.	above 7	21 22

Performance Criteria for WRITTEN EXPRESSION	Level	Mark
Some of the pupils' ideas are clearly expressed. The basic grammatical structure of some sentences is correct and some punctuation is used accurately. The spelling of simple words is usually accurate and the handwriting is mostly legible, though there may be obvious weaknesses in the formation of some letters.	- below 4 +	1 2 3
Pupils' ideas are generally clear with some appropriate organisation. Sentence structures and vocabulary are beginning to be used effectively to develop a point of view. Punctuation to mark sentences is mostly used accurately and pupils are beginning to use punctuation within the sentence. The spelling of simple and common polysyllabic words is generally accurate. Handwriting is mostly clear and legible.	- 4 +	4 5 6
Pupils' writing is clearly expressed and usually organised into a straightforward structure or paragraphs. Vocabulary and sentence structures are sometimes chosen effectively to clarify and develop their point of view, but may not be maintained convincingly throughout. A range of punctuation, including commas, apostrophes and quotation marks is usually used accurately. Spelling, including that of words with complex regular patterns, is usually accurate. Handwriting is generally clear and legible in a fluent style.	- 5 +	7 8 9
Pupils' writing is clear, structured and mostly in an appropriate style for a discursive piece. The use of vocabulary and grammatical structures, together with appropriate paragraphing, contribute to the clarity of the writing though the same quality may not be evident throughout. A range of punctuation is usually used correctly to clarify meaning. Spelling is accurate, though there may be some errors in difficult words. Handwriting is in a fluent and legible style.	- 6 +	10 11 12
Pupils' writing is confident and organised, and it is in an appropriate style although it may be unsophisticated in tone at times. Ideas are developed by a range of grammatical features and the effective use of vocabulary. Paragraphing and punctuation are used to make the sequence of ideas clear. Spelling, including that of complex irregular words, is correct. Handwriting is in a fluent and legible style.	- 7 +	13 14 15
Pupils' writing presents arguments clearly in a coherent way. The choice of style and structure, supported by the precise use of vocabulary and grammatical structures, enables clarity and emphasis to be achieved. Pupils show a consistent grasp of the correct use of paragraphing and a range of punctuation. Spelling, including that of complex irregular words, is correct. Handwriting is in a fluent and legible style.	above 7	16